An Unbe[lievable Guide]
to Rapid, Remarkable Change

bright mind
happy heart
best life

Deanna LoTerzo

Be Ever Curious!
Deanna ♡

◆ FriesenPress

One Printers Way
Altona, MB R0G 0B0
Canada

www.friesenpress.com

Copyright © 2022 by Deanna LoTerzo
www.deannaloterzo.com
First Edition — 2022

All rights reserved.

No part of this publication may be reproduced in any form, or by any means, electronic or mechanical, including photocopying, recording, or any information browsing, storage, or retrieval system, without permission in writing from FriesenPress.

The author of this book does not dispense medical advice or prescribe the use of any technique as a treatment for physical, emotional, or mental problems without the advice of a physician, either directly or indirectly. The intent of the author is only to offer information of a general nature to help you in your quest for emotional and spiritual well-being. In the event you use any of the information in this book for yourself, which is your constitutional right, the author and the publisher assume no responsibility for your actions.

ISBN
978-1-03-911923-9 (Hardcover)
978-1-03-911922-2 (Paperback)
978-1-03-911924-6 (eBook)

1. *Self-Help, Personal Growth*

Distributed to the trade by The Ingram Book Company

Table of Contents

Introduction ... ix

biography becomes biology

Chapter 1: It's Not a Coincidence ... 3
Chapter 2: Embracing Change ... 11
Chapter 3: New Dimensions ... 17
Chapter 4: Your Brilliant Brain ... 31

tips, tools, and techniques

Chapter 5: Discovering Your World ... 53
Chapter 6: Accessing Your Creative Genius ... 67
Chapter 7: Emotions, Attributes, and Feelings ... 87
Chapter 8: Misguided Thinking and Core Beliefs ... 115

freedom from deception and disinformation

Chapter 9: Reclaim Your Identity and Self-Esteem ... 139
Chapter 10: No More Secrets: Surviving the Aftermath of Abuse ... 171
Chapter 11: De-Mystifying Eating Disorders and Weight Loss ... 191
Chapter 12: Embracing the Flow of Money and Abundance ... 211
Chapter 13: Advanced Integration Scripts ... 225
Chapter 14: Our World of Oneness ... 245
For Practitioners and Workshop Facilitators:
    Bright Mind, Happy Heart Workshops / Courses ... 249

Resources ... 251
About the Author ... 255

This book is dedicated to…

*My brother John, my guiding light,
with love and gratitude beyond words.*

My dear friend and kindred creative spirit, Cathy McKernan, without whom this book would never have seen the light of day. I am grateful beyond measure to have the benefit of your wise words, humor, and unwavering support. My life is infinitely richer because you are in it.

The many clients and students who have allowed me to share their journey, contributed their experiences to this book, and encouraged me to take this program to a broader audience.

*"All our dreams can come true,
if we have the courage to pursue them."*

Walt Disney

Introduction

If you've learned to accept the unacceptable, have lost all confidence in yourself, believe that your goals and aspirations are too far from reach, or that lasting change is not possible, then this book is for you. With a deeper understanding of your body's innate healing capacities and defense mechanisms, you will be able to rapidly alter your mindset and brighten your vision, whatever the starting point. For generations, we have been taught to believe that we have minimal control over our physical, emotional, and psychological health – that our DNA's genetic inheritance is our destiny, ironclad, and unalterable. That notion has finally been debunked due to the efforts of a global consortium of biologists, geneticists, and neuroscientists whose discoveries have led to an unprecedented departure from the theory that nature triumphs over nurture.

These revolutionary discoveries provide irrefutable evidence of the extent to which we are profoundly influenced by our environment, beliefs, and emotions. It shows how we are all endowed with an instinctive intelligence to heal, learn, and expand our consciousness. The guidance in this book will rekindle your innate abilities to problem-solve and form meaningful connections with others as you consciously make life-affirming choices the foundation of your new reality. For those who are unrelentingly curious and optimistic, that's good news. It's only bad news for those who still blame their maladaptive behaviors, moods, and tantrums on others.

Let's dive right in. Emotions, feelings, thoughts, and beliefs are a form of intangible energy – much like electricity, which is fluid, multi-directional, and harnessed for diverse purposes. It's not something we think about often, even though subconscious thoughts and emotions account for over 90% of our interactions with the external world, every day. Typically, they claim attention only when our routines, relationships, and lifestyle are either rudely interrupted by disappointing or unwanted events, or by happy accidents and other life-affirming experiences. Something as simple as doing or being the recipient of an act of kindness can totally change the way you feel and think – in an instant. Think about it. What that means on a grander scale is that constructive interplay, creative ideas, and inspired solutions can also be communicated as effectively.

I was reminded of that fact and its potential, while sitting up in my hospital bed, post-surgery, reflecting on life – as one does when faced with a not-so-optimistic prognosis. I wondered what I could do to reverse the outcome. The idea that I could be proactive in my post-surgical treatment plan, instead of reliant on traditional methods, was radical and overwhelming at first. I seriously doubted that I would make it. Still, the thought persisted. What emerged was a plausible plan to reverse-engineer the emotional trauma I had experienced since early childhood and which continued to undermine my mental and physical health. When that plan settled into my bones, I felt inspired and optimistic.

Here's my reasoning. From neurobiologists, we learn that sensations relayed from our senses inwards to our brain and throughout the nervous system travel at speeds up to 270 miles per hour. That's

INTRODUCTION

faster than a blink of an eye. It made sense to me that those same systems can function in reverse to *release* misguided thoughts, limiting beliefs, and corrosive emotions — and at the same rate. Why not? The fact that I am still here is testament to that reality. If you're not having a WOW moment right now, you should be! You are probably asking yourself: *If this is true, why are we not doing it?* The answer, in a nutshell, is this priceless gem from Albert Einstein, and he should know: "We cannot solve our problems with the same thinking we used when we created them."

Bright Mind, Happy Heart, Best Life **heals and transforms lives.** It shares my unique program of mindful tools and techniques that take you down the path of self-exploration and transformation using a powerful series of comprehensive glossaries which interpret emotion and behavior. Through them, misguided thoughts, self-sabotaging behaviors, and corrosive emotions are replaced by life-affirming options to support your new goals and direction, enabling you to live as the luminous being you were born to be. The key to its effectiveness is its *simplicity*. It's not complicated. It's proven. Results are immediate and lasting.

The reason many self-help programs and positive-thinking books largely disappoint is that they totally disregard the need to lay a proper foundation for sustainable change. I use the analogy of gardening. For a new season of growth and new seeds to take firm hold, soil needs to be free of weeds and other impediments that limit the seeds' capacity to germinate. Only then are we rewarded with vibrant colorful blooms. In the same way, weeding all that ails you in order to seed new thought patterns and optimism is empowering and freeing beyond imagination. It means you no longer need to be defined by your past mistakes, guilt, fears, and other corrosive emotions. You do not have to feel hopeless or helpless ever again, or feel like a victim.

You will soon discover what it feels like to enjoy fuller freedom of expression without being limited by false perceptions or triggered by certain people or circumstances. It means that you will have creative control over the evolution of your future and that of your loved ones. There's no going back. Even better news is that it will take you no longer than a day to get your head around the process and to see real results. Rapid, radical, and lasting transformation is what I'm offering, *not* a quick or temporary fix. That's a promise.

As a life coach, I've had the privilege of sharing the contents of this book with countless others for over eighteen years. Its effectiveness is evidenced by endorsements from workshop participants, private clients, and health professionals whose lives have been transformed well beyond expectation or recognition, as has my own. It worked regardless of their starting point and without unwanted side effects. I share their stories and my own throughout the book as evidence of what is truly possible. Empowered, resilient, and self-assured, each is now aligned to their deeper nature. With newfound clarity of thought, more effective problem solving, and a heightened sense of well-being, new creative goals are being achieved and surpassed. Self-destructive habits are a thing of the past. Broken, unfulfilling, or abusive relationships have been cast aside, often with loving kindness, or healed and strengthened. New loving and nurturing relationships are firmly anchored. Fractured families and friendships have become more cohesive, respectful, and accepting; work-related challenges have been more easily and appropriately addressed and overcome. For them, life is just easier and more satisfying. They are freer and more expressive, knowing they are in control of a vibrant, happier future.

Here's what you can expect from this book. It's most likely going to be a huge paradigm shift in more ways than one. Within the first four chapters, you'll discover little-known game-changing facts that will amaze you. I've incorporated those into simple, easy-to-learn exercises to start the process of laying new creative pathways in your brilliant brain. The tools and scripts you'll learn are so simple that at first you won't believe they can be effective. You'll be surprised at being able to initiate profound change in the space of a few minutes.

Please take special note of this next sentence because it is vitally important and fundamental to your success. Working effectively with these tools will come easily *only* when you lay down the need for control and surrender to the idea of *simplicity*. That is the key. Set aside all conditioning that favors complex, hard-learned, and rigid solutions. None of that applies here. The more you over-think it, the less likely you will be to achieve your goals. Children find the creative process so easy because they are less conditioned to be skeptical; they jump right in and let their imaginations run wild. That's how it's done. In that state of mind, the changes you make are proven to be rapid, effective, and lasting. So, if you are ready to heal your old wounds and discover new ways of thinking and being, let's start over.

ABOUT THIS BOOK

Part 1: Biography Becomes Biology lays the foundation for everything that follows. I share a few momentous decisions that changed my life in every way, in the hope that you too will be inspired and courageous enough to push through your fears and rigid beliefs. Then, there's proof that you are born with innate abilities to make sustainable change – even though you don't *really* believe you can, and you worry what that might look like. Also, in this section you will be introduced to eye-opening findings of biologists, geneticists, and experts who interpret the existence of our body's inherent creative and healing capabilities, which some refer to as attributes of our "superhuman" self. Well managed, they will change the trajectory of your life. Following that chapter is an introduction to your brain, which along with an ever-beating and loving heart, ought to be acknowledged as your most prized possession. There's also tips on how to optimize your mental and emotional health in fun and creative ways.

Part 2: Tips, Tools, and Techniques proves the potential of an exciting new future. Those chapters provide you with the nuts and bolts of how and why a "weed and seed" approach works most effectively. They offer practical tools and scripts you can use lifelong. Powerful, inspiring narratives from client files are supported by a few practical exercises to help you connect to your unique truth. Think of these exercises as you would a pre-game warmup, preparing you to get the very best of your mind, body and spirit. Chapters 7 and 8 are vitally important and powerful. This is where the rubber meets the road. Here's where you will learn how to play creatively with conscious intention to rapidly reprogram your subconscious thoughts and emotions. One of the most exciting things that will occur is that you will *immediately* feel something happening to your body, mind, and spirit, as you start using the scripts. Some of the most dramatic transitions I've had the privilege to witness emerged from these chapters.

INTRODUCTION

Part 3: Freedom from Deception and Disinformation addresses the consequences of specific incidental or ongoing trauma. Alongside inspiring client stories are unique tools and other valuable insights. Chapters include Reclaim Your Identity and Self-Esteem, No More Secrets: Surviving the Aftermath of Abuse, De-Mystifying Eating Disorders and Weight Loss, and Embracing the Flow of Money and Abundance. These are followed by advanced integration tools and exercises in Chapter 13.

While I appreciate your enthusiasm for a miraculous, immediate transition to your best life, I strongly recommend that you *master* the core work first in all chapters up to and including Chapters 7 and 8. This way, you will have a better understanding of how various aspects of the program fit together to complement each other and best support your needs and intentions. What I want for you, with all my being, is the most rapid, effective, and lasting transformation, and that will only happen if you act on this advice.

Based on a long-running series of successful workshops, this book is proven. It's also easy to read, without hard-to-understand or hard-to-implement ideas. It's interactive and well researched. I've included established findings and wisdom of experts in a concise way. You don't have to read forty to fifty books and search countless websites to find your way. Everything you need is here.

I hope your creative spark is ignited, and you are excited to regain control of your life, as I did. Now, *as happy as a clam*, I'm living in optimal health and joy on the other side of what the world said I should do and be. My work and my life are vibrant, productive, and meaningful – way beyond my best expectation. You can do the same.

Now is the moment to decide if you truly want to embrace your full potential – or continue as you are, barely coping and having only fleeting glimpses of happiness mingled with chaos, stress, and uncertainty. My heartfelt wish is that you join me so that your life might also be filled with wonder, wisdom, and wellness.

Namaste
Deanna LoTerzo

biography becomes biology

*"All truth passes through three stages.
First, it is ridiculed. Second, it is violently opposed.
Third, it is accepted as self-evident."*

Arthur Schopenhauer

Chapter 1

It's Not a Coincidence

I've learned to notice and respond optimistically when a series of so-called coincidences happen, particularly if they happen in a condensed time frame. The first out-of-the-blue conversation about Nepal was with a janitor in my office, late one evening. She'd been absent for almost two months, so I asked if she had been unwell. "No, thanks for asking. I've been volunteering in an orphanage in Nepal, which I do every other year. This janitorial job pays for my trip, then I come back to it." She went on to tell me more about her passion for helping the kids and her commitment to making a difference in the world. I remember thinking, *How wonderful it must be to have that freedom.* Until then, what I knew of Nepal was limited to travel advertisements luring tourists to Kathmandu, its capital, as an exotic vacation destination.

Within a week, I found myself in conversation with the principal of the holistic health clinic where I was providing psychotherapy services on a part-time basis. I'd known him for years, without him ever mentioning that he spent weeks of his honeymoon exploring Nepal.

Then, within three weeks, I heard from a client I had expected to see sooner, but hadn't. When he called to schedule an appointment, he explained that a group of friends had invited him to go trekking in Nepal. An avid trekker and traveler, he shared that: "Nowhere I've been before can compare to this trip and trekking the Annapurna Trail. It was the most physically and emotionally challenging I've ever had." You get where I'm going with this. I was intrigued.

Early one morning, shortly after, I received a vision, which felt more like a prompt that I would be going to Nepal. However, I immediately dismissed it as an improbability due to work commitments. In the months following, curiosity turned to possibility and finally became acceptance, even though Nepal was not on my bucket list. Hawaii was. Mentioning the prospect to friends, I received enthusiastic support; mentioning it to my family had the complete opposite effect, albeit well-intentioned. "Seriously? Having just recovered from cancer, you are thinking of going to a third-world country on your own…about which you know nothing…with very little likelihood of there being adequate medical facilities?" Their concerns became mine. I soon became galvanized by fear.

From then on, when my inner voice prompted a move forward to prepare for my journey, I refused point blank. My fear-driven dialogue went something like this: *Thanks for the opportunity, but I'm not going. I don't fancy going there on my own. I can ill afford an extended unpaid sabbatical. It would be impossible to find a tenant who wants a flexible lease. I don't speak Nepali or Tibetan, and most likely my food allergies will pose an insurmountable challenge. That should do it.*

For months, I was either tormented by fear, stuck in the limbo of indecision, or totally gripped by the potential and exhilaration of a new adventure. Very slowly, I softened, succumbed, and started to prepare. As a typical Type A personality, avid planner, and organizer, every possible and unforeseen eventuality was covered. Then, much to my own and others' complete surprise, instead of taking an extended leave of absence, having completely surrendered to my inner guidance, I resigned from my full-time role as state director of a national, service-based organization and the comfortable future I'd planned. The next day, sheer panic set in. *What are you doing? You love your lifestyle.*

Among my guilty pleasures were the comforting aromas and flavors of warm fruity Merlot, rich dark Belgian chocolate, and authentic French pastries. I also admit to a fetish for imported designer t-shirts, and designer anything, in natural fibers. Oh, I forgot…the shoe fetish. In my downtime, I played golf with a passion and thoroughly enjoyed Saturday competitions with a lively group of equally competitive women. I had traveled to Europe a few times, been seduced by the intrigue and romance of Paris, spent a disagreeable week in an ever-bustling Hong Kong, and had visited the United States for work. A long-awaited detour to Disneyland in Anaheim was a dream come true – the chance to visit the Disney characters who were part of my fondest childhood memories. Another item on my bucket list checked, and more to come. That was the plan. Now, here I was sitting alone in my apartment, unemployed, plane ticket to Kathmandu in hand, torn between a justifiable fear of the unknown and the incredible intoxication of it.

It's good to know the Universe has a sense of humor. Let's take a little step back. While waiting for my new passport, I was *really* put to the test when offered "the job of a lifetime". I was ecstatic and tempted, if only briefly, to rejoin the team of highly talented people who I'd worked with for the past seven years. The role was everything I had aspired to and more. It offered a comfortable life and safe alternative to what I was contemplating. Thankfully, the voice from my heart spoke louder than the one in my head.

In preparing for my journey, I'd expected to be guided by a well-defined agenda and clarity about what I should be looking for or what was expected of me. It's what I was used to, what kept me together. It wasn't forthcoming. So, I flew out of Brisbane airport armed only with an intuitive sense that I was to be more open to the same sort of momentum that had brought me to this point. Easier said than done. Knowing that, I allowed myself seven days of orientation in Kathmandu. I had made no advance bookings for additional accommodation and didn't have any set plans. I understood my challenge was to learn to trust my guidance and intuitive capacity; that I needed to make a permanent shift from a lifestyle of logic, discipline, and always "doing" and move towards a more fluid, intuitive existence, one of just "being". In order to be completely responsive to whatever circumstances arose, this also meant that there was to be no pre-determined time frame for my stay. I'd know when it was time to return.

Nothing can prepare you for the harsh reality of living conditions in a developing country. It was distressing beyond words. I had taken the physical conditions, safety, abundance of food, and other trappings of my existence totally for granted. Bearing witness to the locals' daily struggle with hunger, poverty, and instability fueled by the Maoist rebellion, I was overcome by profound sadness. Ten days into my sabbatical, heartbroken, physically ill and feverish, I took to my bed, slept fitfully, ate nothing, and cried endlessly. I decided to ship out as soon as I was able. Whatever was intended for me here was not going to happen.

Still confined to my bed four days later, I experienced a radical shift in consciousness; my despair had lifted. I understood there would be no point in abandoning what I came to refer to as *my assignment*. The to-do list would still be waiting for me at some other place and time. So, I had best get myself together and get on with it. From then on, surrendering to the unknown with only curiosity, I was rewarded with the most amazing and unpredictable experiences, insights, and joy beyond imagination.

One such an unplanned experience, certainly one of the highlights of my journey was my extended stay at a Buddhist monastery. Although I am not a Buddhist, nor did I have any intention of becoming one, I enrolled in the winter program for Studies of Buddhist Philosophy. I joined a class of almost forty other Western devotees and was warmly welcomed. Somewhere in between a rigorous class schedule and meditation practice, we shared a mutual curiosity and many discussions about the commonalities and differences between Spiritualism and Buddhist philosophies. The environment was ideal for the task at hand.

Usually in the mornings, in my free time, I would sit in the smaller of the two shrine rooms, pen in hand, requesting Universal guidance as to what was needed. Just being there in the stillness with no external distractions allowed information downloads to happen fluidly, instantaneously, and with perfect clarity. Propped up on a stack of meditation cushions to keep from the cold, white marble floor and wrapped warmly in pashmina shawls in the winter months, I filled many pages of my journals. In those sittings, which could take up to two or three hours, I was committed to fix whatever was broken and hurt, and to realign my beliefs and behaviors.

Sometimes, funny things happened. Often, I was blessed to be joined by the shrine room's curator – a shy, mid-aged monk who was always smiling and enjoyed drumming as part of his daily rituals. As endearing as he was, I initially found the drumming to be as irritating as nails scaping a chalk-board, but after a while, the gentle, steady rhythm accelerated my own healing process, and it became comforting. Then, I found myself looking forward to my daily visits to the shrine room – that is, until he very kindly insisted, in Tibetan, that I join him in a cup of hot tea with yak butter to warm me during our early-morning rituals. Let's just say that I was saved from a repeat experience with the help of a Tibetan-speaking Westerner who negotiated yak-free tea going forward.

Intuitively, seven months after landing at Tribhuvan International Airport, Kathmandu, it was time to go. I was changed, beyond any doubt, at the most profound level. A heightened self-awareness had emerged, as did acceptance of self and others without judgment. I felt cleansed, calmer, lighter, stronger, less angry and defensive, and much more compassionate. An unmistakable sense of purpose, fearlessness, and clarity had settled into my bones. Core values and beliefs continued to shift, as I felt profound gratitude and appreciation for my quality of life. I was humbled by it. I arranged to meet my sister and niece in London and flew directly to Heathrow. Having been all but physically reconfigured in Nepal, confrontation with the harsh reality of a crowded, bustling London was a huge culture shock. On return to Australia a few months later, I sold my apartment and chattels and relocated to Canada.

The life I lead now is, by choice, much simpler and less cluttered and founded upon an enduring inner peace. To this day, the benefits of my sabbatical in Nepal continue to unfold and surprise. Needless to say, imported designer t-shirts are no longer high on my list of "must haves" for a happy, fulfilling life.

By the way, our spiritual guidance is just that – guidance. It's not a command. We are all blessed with the ability to make a conscious choice, whatever the circumstance.

BEFORE YOU MOVE ON...

Have there been times in your life when you have felt intuitively pointed in a specific direction? Did you act in alignment with that guidance? If so, write down the consequences. If not, and you have harbored regret about that choice, write the reasons why you feel regretful.

Chapter 2

Embracing Change

We each have a unique story that influences the way we interpret and negotiate the world around us and our relationships. The emotional imprint of that journey and the expression of it is reflected in our willingness and capacity to manage future challenges and to adapt successfully to change. Does the mere prospect of change create overwhelming fear and distress for you or an exhilarating surge of anticipation?

You have a choice. When you choose fear as your response, the consequences are typically self-destructive, unless it is a genuine "fight or flight" situation. If you are attuned to your body when fear arises, you will be aware of a tightening in mind and body as tension escalates; then a sense of being stuck and unable to move forward – not only in relation to the problem at hand, but also in other aspects of your life. You become more cautious and tentative in the decision-making process and often start questioning whether you have ever had the capacity to make positive, life-affirming choices. As fear and stagnation set in to define you, molehills become mountains, and you inadvertently place yourself at risk of serious ill-health.

Until recently, the idea that emotions and thoughts directly impact physiology, specifically the immune system, was not understood. However, recent innovations in biotechnology now enable scientists to see that the immune, endocrine, and nervous systems are interwoven and in a constant state of interplay, and that perceptions as well as emotions shape our immune system.

Psychologically and emotionally, living in fear generates a sense of being small and not in control of our lives. In that state of being, we further risk becoming susceptible to the control and manipulation of others. Fear causes stagnation, disappointment, confusion, and helplessness; it begets even more fear and resistance to change.

CHANGE AS AN ADVENTURE

I was no different from anyone else when confronted unexpectedly by changed circumstances. The familiar represents safety, security, and comfort. So why do we need to change? And how can we process change in a positive, constructive way?

Sometimes, the burden of our familiar past weighs like an anchor – even though it may be filled with happy memories.

Look around. Our present-day reality is that "life is change". We are living in times of profound technological advancement, the capability to connect to people across the globe with only a few clicks, ongoing political upheaval, and new discoveries in both epigenetics and neuroscience that have forever changed our perspective on health and well-being. And yet, we continue to adapt and respond organically because it is in our very nature to do so. Those influences seep quietly into our mindset and daily grind, accepted as our new reality.

From the moment we are born, we become responsive to both our internal and external environments. As an infant, we respond instinctively to our mother's proximity and her voice: we hear it, are comforted by it, and feel safe. We begin experimenting with the potential benefits of expression by crying incessantly when our needs are not being met. Not only do we adapt at that young age, but we also become creative in our efforts to manipulate the outcomes.

Within the first twelve months, we are typically able to recognize and differentiate between female and male voices and facial features; we learn to categorize and acclimatize to a shifting landscape. Curious, we approach the transition from crawling to walking independently with sheer excitement. It's a joy to watch. We ache to explore what's beyond – to touch it, feel it, talk to it, and probe – always pushing, testing the boundaries of our ever-expanding capacities. Everyday life becomes a new adventure, curiosities are satisfied, and momentous milestones are met and overcome with increasing self-confidence.

Have you ever seen a toddler try, time and again, to climb from the floor to the sofa? Their focus, creativity, and determination are inspiring. When finally they arrive, the look of triumph and its message is undeniable: "Look at me. I'm awesome! What's next?"

As life progresses and circumstances change, we forget we have emerged from the womb with all the tools needed to support our transition to adulthood. I'm here to remind you that you are endowed with an amazing array of character traits that are at risk of remaining dormant – unless you make a conscious effort to incorporate their expression into your daily routines. Amongst those instinctive qualities are compassion, courage, authenticity, creativity, curiosity, optimism, spontaneity, determination, self-confidence, and a sense of fun – all aspects of profound wisdom. When allowed to flourish, those elements empower us to live productive, interesting, and rewarding lives, all the while seeking "what's next?"

In truth, *change is the only way forward*, although sometimes at the outset it may not appear so. It may present at the "wrong" time, be on a grander scale than you think you can cope with, result from a surprise or shock, or be expected but unquestionably unwelcome.

To quote Oprah Winfrey: "Turn your wounds into wisdom." Using the pandemic as an example, let's acknowledge the many silver linings that have emerged from this crisis. Individually and collectively, we have become more reflective than distracted, more kind than critical, more accepting than divisive, more patient than intolerant, more adaptable than rigid, and more deliberate in our thoughts and actions. We have redirected our attention to what matters most – our families, our health, and well-being. We've learnt educational and playful ways to be with our children, discovered long dormant creative abilities, developed new skill sets and fitness routines, and enjoyed healthier dietary habits. It's proof positive that we are inherently wired to adapt to a changing environment, whatever the circumstances.

The following page contains a diagram, the Formation of Response Patterns, which is a snapshot of life's interactive events and their potential consequences.

Whatever the circumstance, you have a choice in how to respond. Retreating to a place of fear is not the ideal choice; it merely serves to slow your progress and suppress your immune system. Acceptance of the new reality is a reasonable starting point. A quiet, or even optimistic, curiosity is preferred. Even better would be a sense of excitement about the potential of forward momentum, accompanied by the kind of creative thinking that will produce only the best potential outcome.

Remember that you have a lifetime of adaptive experience supporting you. So, when change is looming, take the chance: e*mbrace it and live as the person you were born to be!*

BEFORE YOU MOVE ON...

How do you routinely respond to change? Are you curious, excited, and motivated? Or are you likely to avoid it, gently resist, or get dragged into it screaming? If fear is your response, do you have any idea why change has become problematic? What happened to suppress your innate curiosity?

FORMATION OF RESPONSE PATTERNS

LIFE EVENTS	HELD IN SUBCONSCIOUS MEMORY	GOVERN FUTURE RESPONSE
Interpretation of Life Events is Influenced by	*Initiate New or Reinforce Pre-Established*	*Your Choice of Response Determines*
|	|	|
Family & Ancestral Traditions	Core Beliefs Attitudes Habits	If You Remain Stuck, Confused & Unhappy
|	|	|
Cultural Norms & Expectations	Feelings, Moods Emotional Inventory	Living As A Victim Of Past Events or People
|	|	|
Social & Peer Group Pressure Collective Consciousness	Maladaptive Or Appropriate Behavioral Response	OR *LIVE AS YOUR TRUE SELF -*
|	|	*VIBRANT,*
Self-Imposed Vows, Oaths Agreements	Healthy Emotional Engagement Or Unhealthy Attachment Or Addiction	*CREATIVE, & HAPPIER!*
|		
Past or Parallel Life Cycles Alternate Realities		

Chapter 3

New Dimensions

The life-changing epiphany that led to the publication of this book occurred while I was in the hospital just two days after surgery to remove a rapidly growing breast tumor. Why was I the only one in my family to fall victim to this disease? My cancer-free siblings and I shared the same Italian heritage, were reared on a healthy, hearty European diet (with a particular fondness for cheese, pasta, and fresh-baked bread), and wanted for nothing materially. What clearly distinguished my life from theirs was our chosen paths – theirs to marriage and child-rearing, mine to an interesting career and a confusing, hopelessly single existence. Unlike my siblings, I struggled through my teens and early adult years with the emotional intelligence of a gnat. More about that later. Time and again, any chance at potential happiness was torn to shreds by betrayal and humiliation, adding to an already profound sense of worthlessness. That's what I came to expect, and that's what materialized, repeatedly. With my belief system shaken to its core and emotions shattered, there I was in that hospital bed, feeling sad and sorry.

Then, the epiphany. What do I know as fact? The rate at which energetic impulses travel around the body, and that every action has an equal, opposite reaction. I decided to apply those principles to unravel the emotional mess that was my life and to hopefully heal my mind and body. Within hours of making that decision I found a way. Sure, it needed some refinement to become what you are reading about today, but in my short time remaining in the hospital, I felt a shift happening. I was off to a good start.

There was a lot to do. Emotions such as grief, sadness, loneliness, rejection, shame, disappointment, and outrage, stored and compacted over decades, had served as a defense mechanism for way too long. I persisted in my efforts to "weed" them out. The term "weeding" fit well with my intentions. The first to go were feelings of confusion and being overwhelmed, which sat like an umbrella protecting the rest. Those two feelings consistently fueled the misconceptions that *I can't do this,* and *I am unworthy of a different life.* They had to go. By far the most challenging aspect of converting my intentions into a simple, practical transitional process was to trust in what I believed possible. It wasn't as simple as saying, "I *really* want to be happy" and expecting the intention alone to reverse decades of pain, trauma, and abuse. That's too broad, too generic. I experienced the most immediate and effective results when I kept the phrasing simple, yet specific, and I broke the broader picture into snapshots.

Then I discovered the core belief that *any attempt to heal on my own terms would have fatal consequences.* I questioned if I had the courage and capacity to commit to the alternative therapies I was contemplating. Clearing those blocks was a major turning point, enabling me to make choices I would not have previously considered. Without those therapies, I can say with complete conviction that I would not be here today living in vibrant health and sharing my story. Refusing to succumb to my surgeon's insistence upon traditional post-surgical treatments, I continued my journey of self-discovery and healing. I was given twenty-four months to live as a consequence of that choice. I made steady, unmistakable progress based on nothing other than blind faith, intention, and the belief that emotion and thoughts are fluid and reversible. Of course, I suffered through bad days wondering if I'd made the right choice, but gradually they were fewer and fewer as I came to accept the unassailable truth that I was in control of my future.

The sole purpose of this book is to share with you, dear reader, the most important truths you will ever learn. Perhaps you already know them and have forgotten, or have taken them for granted. I said this earlier, but I really feel the need to stress that: *when you truly understand and accept what is possible, you will never again settle for anything less.*

The scientific proof of why and how our body is inherently wired to respond rapidly and effectively to change was the subject of my next research project; the specifics of which are covered in the following pages. It might seem like an overwhelming amount of information, and some concepts may not resonate initially; you may require more time for contemplation to align your head and your heart. These revelations will bring perspective and order to your mind and a sense of control over your life. You will also feel less fearful as the potential of a brighter reality becomes accessible.

So, I encourage you to read on because you will be astounded by the discoveries that have caused even the most rigid and conservative scientific minds to readjust their notions of what is now both real and possible in our natural world.

To begin, let's get your every-day reality into perspective. Simply put, the pivotal influences upon your state of wellness and life circumstances are multiple:

- Your genetic makeup and predisposition
- Your programmed beliefs and the emotions that anchor them
- Your food and any other ingested substances
- Your immediate family, ancestry, and external relationships
- Your culture and sociological history
- The vast ocean of vibrational quantum energy that surrounds and connects us all

We are a composite of those fluid, ever-changing elements. This multi-dimensional definition of your life may appear initially to be daunting, but won't once you realize (as I did) that in transforming your core beliefs and their emotional roots, you have ultimate control over all other influences. You can decide what you will and will not accept as an integral part of your life and your future, and discard anything that no longer serves, regardless of your starting point. There is no doubt that what follows will have an impelling effect on your mindset and worldview. Though, mostly what you need, in addition to the data, is *an open mind* and the courage to confront whatever impediment is keeping you from reaching your full potential.

THE BASELINE – GENETIC INHERITANCE 101

Genetic inheritance is the concept with which we are most familiar, so we will start there and then to trace the less familiar scientific advances in chronological order.

"Genetic determinism" is the term given to the Darwinian theory that our destiny, our health, and susceptibility to disease are inherited directly through our DNA (deoxyribonucleic acid), which acts as the blueprint for building our bodies and reproductive systems. In humans, DNA contained in the nucleus of each cell is comprised of forty-six chromosomes (twenty-three from the mother and twenty-three from the father) residing within a structure called a double helix. DNA is also responsible indirectly for the formation of proteins, which are the major structural component of all cells, especially muscles. As the blueprint for construction, it determines whether you will have blue, brown, or hazel eyes; a tall or short stature; blond or dark hair; fair or dark skin; and dimples or just an engaging smile. This theory argued that nature triumphs over nurture; that our DNA's genetic inheritance was our destiny and iron-clad and unalterable.

In the past decade or so, with rapid advances in biotechnology, the concept of genetic determinism has been successfully challenged. We now know that DNA is constantly subject to mutations – accidental and random changes in its code. Mutations can lead to missing or malformed cellular proteins, which can lead to disease. Most important is that recent discoveries prove mutations also can be caused by exposure to *environmental factors* including chemicals, UV radiation, foods and the chemicals used in food processing, smoking, or other toxins included in everyday household items.

So, what happened next? A shift in quantum consciousness.

QUANTUM CONSCIOUSNESS

It was the momentous work of Niels Bohr, Max Planck, and Albert Einstein in the field of quantum physics that revolutionized traditional thinking about the composition of matter and its form and function; time and space; the multidirectional flow of energy; and the potential of parallel realities. Quantum theory laid the groundwork for unparalleled scientific progress and technological advancement, as it answered many questions left unresolved by classical theorists, scientists, and mathematicians of the previous century. Classical theory, also referred to as Newtonian Theory, was deterministic. It holds that matter, energy, time, and motion are *constant and predictable* based on the past and follow the same fundamental laws of physics explained through the application of mathematics and logic. It also proposes that *we each exist in a microcosm, as an independent and disconnected composite of atoms* that have no effect on each other.

Quantum theory, in stark contrast, asserts that:

- We live in a world of Oneness, connected to everyone around us and the entire universe within a matrix of pulsating electromagnetic energy.
- The elements within this matrix are in a constant state of fluidity, being responsive and interactive.
- We and everything around us is comprised only of subatomic units of energy called "quanta", which can behave as either particles or waves that move multi-directionally.

- The transformation of these units from particles to waves is dependent upon whether those elements are observed (or measured).
- Everything exists as a consequence of our perceptions. (This means that if we can't or won't see it, it doesn't exist for us.)

A PARTICIPATORY UNIVERSE

John Wheeler enrolled at John Hopkins University at age 16 and emerged as a theoretical physicist. Decades later, as a highly esteemed Professor of Physics at Princeton University, he concluded: "The universe does not exist 'out there', independent of us. We are inescapably involved in bringing about that which appears to be happening." Further, he proposed:

- Reality is subjective, conditional upon the perspective of the observer.
- Conscious observation acts as a catalyst for change.
- We can creatively and actively alter our thoughts, choices, and outcomes – it's just a transference of energy.
- Therefore, we are no longer victims or just passive observers.
- We must now accept responsibility for co-creation.
- We are all connected through energy waves and form part of a "Participatory Universe".

We know that our entire bodies are constantly firing in response to our thoughts, emotions, and environmental conditions. When you step up to become empowered in the co-creation of a new reality, you take on the responsibility to manage your thoughts and emotions more mindfully with your future and that of your children and loved ones at the forefront of your mind.

THE GHOST IN YOUR GENES

Some of the earliest published work in modern-day science about environmental influences upon genes and their intergenerational ramifications was provided by Dr. Lars Olov Bygren, Professor Emeritus at Department of Community Medicine and Rehabilitation, Umea University, Sweden, in the 1980s. He was particularly interested in the long-term effects of famine on the families who lived in Norrbotten, a remote county in northern Sweden.

Previous generations in the county had suffered extremely harsh conditions throughout extended periods of famine when crops failed and families starved. In contrast, some years the crops were so unexpectedly abundant that food was readily available for months, and people became over-indulgent. Studying agricultural records, Bygren's team was able to establish the quantity of food available to ancestors in their childhood during those alternating periods of feast and famine.

He wondered whether the fluctuations in food availability in childhood might somehow impact genetic inheritance in future generations. It was an unorthodox idea, given the then prevailing belief that the impact of personal food choices would have an immediate and direct effect only on one's own health and life, not on any new generation. A key finding was that the life expectancy of male grandchildren of grandparents, whose food supply fluctuated from year to year and who had been gluttonous, was significantly shortened. Similar findings impacted female lines.

An astonishing fact emerged from Bygren's research: powerful environmental conditions (in that instance, effects of the famine and threat of death) can seemingly leave an imprint on genetic material such that it side-steps evolutionary code to introduce new attributes or traits, without altering original DNA code; and it can do so within only one generation. This finding was controversial in that it contradicted the deterministic evolutionary theory by Charles Darwin, which holds that evolutionary change takes place only over many generations.

A contemporary of Bygren and sometime collaborator, Professor Marcus Pembrey, FMedSci, Emeritus Professor of Pediatric Genetics at the Academy of Medical Sciences, is a British clinical geneticist. His ground-breaking research during the late 1970s to early 1980s, while at the Institute of Child Health, University College London and later at the University of Bristol, further advanced our understanding of the contributing determinants of common disease. He made the discovery that the *origin* of a genomic imprint explains the variation in symptoms of the disease from one person to another. For example, both Prader-Willi syndrome and Angelman syndrome are genetic disorders attributed to an identical deletion on chromosome 15, yet are not symptomatically identical. In most cases, a deletion attributed to maternal lineage accounted for Angelman syndrome, while a deletion attributed to paternal lineage manifested as Prader-Willi syndrome. Professor Pembrey's research also led him to the realization that human chromosomes are influenced by lifestyle habits and early life stresses that have been genomically imprinted by parents and grandparents. Other than smoking, environmental factors were previously ignored by health practitioners during the diagnostic process. Believing these genomic imprints are increasingly evident, he recommends that family-based medical history be preserved throughout this and in future generations to ensure a more definitive diagnostic process and better-informed treatment.

THE HUMAN GENOME PROJECT

That idea that disease can be greatly influenced by environmental conditions was further endorsed by the findings of scientific researchers from twenty different countries who were engaged over a period of thirteen years in the Genome Project, which came to a close in 2003. Contrary to expectation, the research proved that humans only have 20,500 – 25,000 genes and that there is no specific genetic coding associated with an equally specific set of symptoms, or disease. Their expectation was that the cause of each disease currently known to humans (there are in excess of 200,000 officially recognized diseases) would be traced to a specific recurring flaw, or mutation, within the genetic code. Therefore, all patients with that same mutated gene would present with identical symptoms. If true, that hypothesis would have enabled the development of a "universal" remedy or treatment regime. No such evidence came to light.

Scientists and doctors have since accepted that complex diseases such as cancer, diabetes, and cardiovascular disease, which constitute the majority of health challenges in the United States, have their foundation in the interaction between diverse environmental influences and multiple genetic factors. Overall, the project met its objective in becoming a comprehensive, global database of information and stimulating the growth of biomedical technology and further research into disease prevention.

THE NEW SCIENCE OF EPIGENETICS

With the existence of a cellular imprint acknowledged, the new science of *epigenetics* emerged. It explains the genomic imprint as being housed in an "epigenome" – material which sits above ("epi") the pre-existing DNA blueprint without altering it and that is passed from generation to generation. The epigenome acts to alter gene expression, controlling whether genes switch on or off, and is influenced by factors such as diet, stress, environmental noise, lifestyle choices, smoking, over-eating, and significant life-altering events including our cognitive and emotional response to them. For example, depressed mothers may give birth to children epigenetically affected by their mothers' mental state. Fetal Alcohol Spectrum Disorder is considered to be the combined effects of both genetic predisposition and epigenetic markers.

The same idea applies to the way we inherit as children our parents' or caregivers' core beliefs, attitudes, and behaviors upon which we build our unique personalities. This includes their way of doing things such as dietary preferences, spiritual beliefs, fears and anxieties, work ethic, child-rearing habits, and their worldview. Typically, their normal becomes our normal. But nowhere is any of that pre-designated in our genes. It is an epigenetic influence, or what some refer to as "cellular memory".

THE BIOLOGY OF BELIEF

Fast forward a few years. Having dealt successfully with my illness using the guidelines and exercises prescribed within this book, yet ever curious about the mind-body-spirit equation, I came across the compelling work of Bruce Lipton Ph.D., cell biologist, author, former research scientist, and medical school professor.

His earliest publication, *The Biology of Belief*, speaks to epigenetics in the context of our beliefs. He urges us to become proactive in the conduct of our daily lives by re-aligning our thoughts. Kudos to me, I'd been doing it for years, already! Based on the evidence of epigenetic science, he advocates that we are masters of our destiny, not victims of life, and that we possess an innate capacity to co-create lives of happiness, fulfillment, and enlightenment. His book is an inspirational read. Hailed as "paradigm-busting" and "a milestone for evolving humanity," it reveals "previously unexplored connections between our biology, psychology, and spirituality."

His and other experts' findings pertinent to your progress throughout this book include the awareness that:

- Genes are molecular blueprints used only in construction.
- Less than 2% of the human genome accounts for heredity.
- 98% of what previously was thought to be "junk DNA" are epigenome sequences that act as control switches to either activate or deactivate genes.
- DNA is controlled by signals from inside and outside the cell.
- Environmental influences, beliefs, and emotions serve as the control mechanisms.
- Perceptions transmit signals to the brain, which controls biological function.
- 70% of peoples' thoughts are negative or redundant.
- 95% of life activity has its foundation in the subconscious.

- Positive or negative thoughts have a profound effect on the behavior of genes – only when in harmony with subconscious programming.

ORGAN TRANSPLANTS, PERSONALITY, AND ENERGETIC PROFILES

In no other circumstance has the dramatic impact of epigenetic influence been more evident than in the life stories of organ transplant recipients. Organ transplants of the heart, lungs, liver, pancreas, and intestinal organs have become commonplace as both surgical procedures and the specificity of drugs have become safer and more sophisticated. The intangible blessings of such a gift of life extend to both donor families and recipients in ways neither could have expected nor believed. What I found most interesting in researching this topic were the anecdotes from recipients who experienced both frightening and intriguing side-effects, which have left the medical fraternity scratching their heads, perplexed yet totally in awe. Those experiences we now acknowledge as transmission of the "energetic profile" of the donor – his or her attitudes, interests, food preferences, personality traits, and mannerisms.

In Claire Sylvia's book, *A Change of Heart*, she takes us through her journey as a heart and lung transplant recipient and its unpredictable aftermath. As just one of many examples, due to life-long health problems, her diet had been sensible and healthy, but somewhat restricted. During her recovery, she gradually transitioned pain-free to what she hoped would be a relatively normal life and resumption of her regular diet. Claire was surprised to find herself drawn to and sometimes craving foods she had never enjoyed before, such as green peppers, beer, Snickers bars, and other sweets. More curious and funnier was her experience when "my car practically steered itself to the nearest Kentucky Fried Chicken." That was a first, as she had never bought from fast-food outlets before.

Her new heart also brought changes to her personality; she felt less lonely, freer, and more independent; for the first time, she realized she no longer felt incomplete without a male companion; she became more assertive, almost aggressive; she developed self-assurance and became aware of a more powerful vibrancy within. Friends commented that even her walk had changed to a "swagger"; not all that surprising given her donor was an eighteen-year-old male motorcyclist who had died in a crash. Physically she had more stamina and a lot more energy at fifty, than she'd ever had. The author went on to establish a much-needed support group for donor families and organ recipients and rediscovered her passion for modern dance.

Chapter 4

Your Brilliant Brain

Since I commenced writing this book, we have all been subject to the uncertainty of the global pandemic and its grievous consequences. This chapter has never been more relevant than it is today as we must learn to adapt to ever-changing challenges to our mental and physical health.

Now that we have looked at the surprising ways our genetic makeup is influenced, and have debunked what we were taught to believe about the rigidity of our inherited traits and their consequences, it's time to take a closer look at the internal processes that *you alone* can control to redefine your future – starting now. This chapter gives insight into the way your ingenuous brain and nervous system process sensory information and then instruct your other organs and systems on the appropriate response to maintain body balance through a wide assortment of hormones. Proper balance and flow of those hormones also determine your mood – whether it be happy and productive or depressed and dysfunctional.

The brain is one of the most complex phenomena in the known universe. It contains more (100 billion) nerve cells, called neurons, than there are human beings on the planet (currently 7.8 billion). That's some firepower you have at your disposal! We have yet to design an app or build a machine that comes remotely close to its capabilities, and I doubt we ever will – though Silicon Valley is working hard at it. Probably due to its complexity, most of us (except those who have a scientific interest) see the brain as rather mysterious and inaccessible, so we ignore it or don't give it the respect it is due.

Think about this: from the moment your conscious brain awakens in the morning to the time you go to sleep at night, it is engaged in trillions of calculations and micro adjustments that allow your body to function with fluid and seamless movement. It initiates immune system responses, monitors your body temperature and heart rate, makes thousands of decisions, engages in multiple conversations and interactions with others, and experiences a mixed range of emotional responses – without you ever having to give it a second thought. And, as we already learned, it activates those functions via electrical impulses (signals) that travel at speeds up to 270 miles per hour – which is less than a blink of an eye. Awesome! Although only 2% of total body weight, the brain uses a significant 20% of the body's total energy production.

Despite its obvious genius, our amazing brain remains forgotten unless confronted with physical injury, chronic forgetfulness, or the fear of dementia. Few people spend any time thinking about how to properly nurture their brain and tap into its potential. Accessing your fullest potential is what this book is all about, so please give your brain some respect and love, starting now.

Remember the last time you had some really good news? Perhaps it was getting a promotion at work or unexpectedly great exam results, being accepted at college or university, enjoying mind-blowing sex, falling in love, or seeing your newborn child for the first time. Don't you wish you could bottle that euphoria, that sense of expectation that *anything is possible?* That exuberance is caused by an elevation in your level of *happy* hormones produced by the delicate interaction between your nervous system and your endocrine system. Your happy hormones are just some of the many types of chemical messengers regulating bodily function, mood, and behavior. Their effects are automatic and immediate in both happy circumstances and the opposite.

Equally, when confronted by stressful situations, the endocrine system responds by releasing *stress* hormones to help you cope with the emotional overload. If left unchecked, consistently elevated stress levels will cause you to scramble from one poor decision to the next, leading you to spiral downwards and feel helpless and distanced from your goals. Multiple studies have discovered that incidental or prolonged periods of stress, sleep deprivation, overwork, and the pressure of tight deadlines and childhood trauma have a profound impact on mental health. You will learn more about those and how to manage them mindfully as we go through this chapter.

Being mindful means that you accept responsibility to nurture and protect your brain from any disruptive or damaging influences. It requires that you live each day being deliberate in your choices. To quote the Ancient Greek philosopher, Aristotle: "Choice, not chance, determines your destiny." Feelings of happiness and infectious optimism greatly increase the likelihood of routinely making objective, creative, and life-affirming choices.

NEUROPLASTICITY

Neuroplasticity is the term that refers to our brain's ability to change and adapt as a result of new experiences. Through research with mice and humans, we learn that growth potential of the brain's nerve cells (called neurons), the creation of new synaptic connections (which allow neuronal cells to communicate and strengthen), and the brain's capacity to adapt to new circumstance is lifelong. When we are born, every neuron has an estimated 2,500 synapses; by age three, this has grown to approximately 15,000 synapses.

Throughout life, the process of "synaptic pruning" causes some synapses to die and others to become strengthened *as we have new experiences*. Have you ever taken notice that when the subject you are learning, the book you are reading, or film you are watching really interests you, it's much easier to retain the content? Why? It's because you are emotionally invested, the subject matter resonates with you, and your brain is doing what it is designed to do – firing on all cylinders and creating new or strengthening existing synaptic connections. Historically, the theory was that the older we become, the less flexible our brain and personality are. Further, it was widely accepted that:

1. The brain is hardwired and fundamentally incapable of growth or change.
2. Those born with brain defects or suffering brain injury have no hope of recovery.

In his book, *The Brain that Changes Itself: Stories of Personal Triumph from the Frontiers of Brain Science*, Norman Doidge, M.D., suggests those prior limiting beliefs stemmed from a lack of insight as to what part of the brain responds to stimuli and how this occurs. Research that began in the mid-1900s is now backed by cutting-edge advances in biotechnology that provide an entirely new perspective of the brain and its malleability. It offers proof that "the brain can change its own structure and function through thought and activity." Also, that brain plasticity is reinforced by *open-ended learning and new experiences*, regular physical activity, restful sleep, proper diet, and social contact. That means we can keep our brains vibrant and curious at any age.

This book is a fascinating read, as it introduces the gifted scientists and doctors who made these remarkable discoveries. Without surgery or medications, they have been responsible for the extraordinary progress made by patients who have triumphed over seemingly impossible odds resulting from grievous injury, learning disabilities, and genetic mutations.

The following newly discovered traits of neuroplasticity are important for you to remember:

- Both genetics (nature) and environment (nurture) make a significant contribution to malleability, as does the interaction between them.
- Over your lifetime, billions of neurons and trillions of synapses are created or strengthened when you develop a new life-affirming habit. On the dark side, destructive habits such as addictions are reinforced each time you indulge them.
- Positive change in both *anatomy and behavior* will occur consistently as a result of learning, memory formation, and life experience. Both are altered by damage to the brain.

- Neurodegeneration and a decline in plasticity can occur as a result of an addiction, such as alcoholism or drug abuse; excessive exposure to EMF (radiation) emissions from electronic devices and electric light; and in adverse biochemical conditions.
- Multiple studies prove a link between the formation of brain and other cancers and long-term exposure to EMF emissions.

HOW CAN BRAIN PLASTICITY WORK FOR YOU?

As we go through life, get married, have children, go to work, and become overwhelmed with responsibilities, we tend to fall into repetitive patterns causing neural circuits to grow and be reinforced. On the one hand, they serve us well in helping to get life organized, providing a sense of stability and predictability, reinforcing feelings of safety, and creating a self-identity. But those routines can also become tedious, boring, and self-defeating. We fall into a rut when, for example, our week is too structured and inflexible so that "every Tuesday we have pasta for dinner, Thursday is Chinese take-out, and Sunday is always a roast (the same as Mom and Dad have done since they married)." It's like wearing comfortable old slippers, but the big toe is starting to poke through, and the soles are almost worn to shreds. Even though we have become bored, unhappy, or disillusioned, the thought of changing those self-imposed structures can be fearful.

If that's you, it's time to step outside of your comfort zone, seek new challenges, and become empowered and invigorated. Sure, you may experience what I refer to as "transitional discomfort", but trust me when I say it is short-lived. Even minor changes to routines, habits, and interests make a huge difference to your mood and well-being as new synaptic connections are stimulated. In fact, *one hour of repeated stimulation is all it takes for the number of synaptic connections to double.* It's true. And important. You might want to read that again to make sure you take it in. You can start with really simple changes to shake things up. Maybe take a different route home or to work, try a different food, go watch the kind of movie you typically wouldn't, treat yourself to coffee in a different location, start a journal, learn a new language, try a different type of exercise, join a club, walk around the block anti-clockwise if you usually go clockwise. Your goal is to create a new habit. You will be surprised how your perspective on life will change, as will your mood. Trust me, it *really is this easy* to create new synaptic connections, and it's the key to a brighter outlook, happier future, and sound mental health. Use your imagination. It's fun to do something different while you are becoming unstuck.

IMAGINATION AND CREATIVITY AT PLAY

To start this segment, I'd like to share one of my favorite pertinent quotes from Deepak Chopra: "The best use of Imagination is Creativity. The worst use of Imagination is Anxiety."

Would you be surprised to learn that our brain responds equally to an imagined event as it does to a lived experience? Neuroscientists have found that when the brain is fed a virtual experience, it is accepted as regular incoming information, which triggers the exact same hormonal and physiological responses as a real-time experience. Creating your own event – and all that you aspire to – is simply the turbo-charged version of positive thinking. It's not a new concept, though it is commonly used as a tool by sports coaches, psychologists, psychotherapists, and the like. For example, as major sporting events have become more competitive and material rewards have sky-rocketed beyond all reasoning, the role of the sports psychologist has taken firm hold. In addition to health and fitness providers and traditional coaching of technical game skills and strategy, many individual players add a sports psychologist to their mix. Most of these consultants do not actually go out to the football field, hockey arena, or the golf course. The focus of their sessions is to get the players into a positive, creative state of mind so they are relaxed and capable of visualizing themselves kicking a field goal or sinking a birdie putt to win the tournament.

Engaging only the subconscious, a virtual experience is created and replayed in the calm and quiet of the consultant's office, far removed from the pressures, distractions, and crowds that dominate public appearances. To begin, the process requires detachment from practicalities, structured practice times, and the relentless drive to win, and then complete surrender to a more relaxed, intuitive state of being. With a clear mind, the focus becomes the imagination of a perfect stroke or touchdown – time and again. A successful outcome on the course or football field will present simply as a consequence of the intentional effort preceding it, as it already exists in the subconscious cellular memory.

Scientific proof of this fact, sourced from experiments conducted by a neuroscientist, Dr. Alvaro Pascual-Leone, Professor of Neurology at Harvard Medical School, proved how repetitive practice of five-finger piano exercises over a short time frame, five days to be precise, *created new circuitry* in the brain. Way more exciting were the results of similar experiments where volunteers, instead of playing the piano, were asked to think about playing the same piece of music in their heads, *using only their imagination* of finger movements. Pascual-Leone was astounded to discover that synaptic changes were triggered by the imagined process of playing, to the same degree as those created by the practical exercises. This is yet another testament to the notion that conscious intention has consequences.

ACTIVATING YOUR HAPPY HORMONES

On a subconscious level, our attitudes and behaviors are motivated by either the expectation of rewards and positive reinforcement or the fear of punishment or other undesirable outcomes, though we are mostly unaware of this on a conscious level. These motivations are driven by neurotransmitters and hormones, which are the most influential yet often-overlooked variables in our body *over which we have almost total control.* They can act urgently to steer you away from anything that is bad or threatening or drive you towards things that are good and that make you happy. Mobilized by the brain and endocrine systems, they regulate most bodily functions from heart rate, body temperature, appetite, sleep patterns, sex drive, blood sugar levels, emotions, mood, and behavior to more complex processes such as growth and reproduction. They promote optimal health when in balance and can have life-altering consequences when that balance is disrupted, even slightly.

When we choose to engage in life-affirming activities, our endocrine system spontaneously releases a range of *happy hormones* to reinforce our sense of well-being and happiness. They are triggered when we are inspired to satisfy the hunger for food; find secure, warm shelter; seek a life-partner; socialize with family friends and loved ones; enjoy loving or fun sex; meditate; listen to music; exercise; or just to be curled up at home feeling safe, reading a good book. Each hormone contributes a unique feeling which, when repeated, becomes wired into our brain circuitry as positive associations for future reference.

Dopamine spurs us into action to find what we need and keeps us focused on those goals. We feel the effects of dopamine when we become aware of the potential for a reward. As a neurotransmitter communicating between nerve cells in the brain, it plays a major role in the processes of creativity, concentration, memory, motor function, and muscle tension. Dopamine is triggered by something as small as a favorite snack or by the potential for a larger reward. Let's say you started a new job three months ago and just completed your probationary performance review. You passed with flying colors and were promised an increase in pay at the end of the sixth month, provided you kept up those same performance standards. That sense of accomplishment you feel is stimulated by a surge in dopamine levels that boosts your self-esteem. You were also informed that there would be two new management training positions opening in twelve months and, after your impressive performance review, the human resources coordinator suggested you keep that in mind. You are elated; your dopamine pathway is again reinforced, excited by the future potential. In a nutshell, your brain is flooded with dopamine when you think positive thoughts, smile, laugh, and hug. Who knew?

Logging on to social media has also been shown to activate a surge of dopamine as it seeks the reward of connection to others, though it has a superficial, fleeting effect. It is worth knowing, however, that the levels arising from social media connections do not provide the same calming, happy, satisfying effects of oxytocin and serotonin hormones as those are stimulated only by real-time interaction and bonding. The consequence of "seeking without satisfaction" like the habit of "friending" can result in an overabundance of dopamine, which feels great, but much like a sugar-high, creates mental hyperactivity and reduces our capacity for sustainable single-mindedness.

While too little dopamine can cause cravings for food, low sex drive, feelings of hopelessness, lack of motivation, schizophrenia, and Parkinson's disease, too much is linked to paranoia, social withdrawal, attention-deficit/hyperactivity disorder, and addictions to drugs, alcohol, food, sex, and gambling. Some of the best ways to boost your dopamine levels without supplementation include regular exercise, high-quality sleep, increased exposure to sunlight, regular sex, meditation, listening to instrumental music, and massage.

Endorphins are the natural opiates which have a morphine-like effect by helping to cope with pain or stress while stimulating feelings of happiness, pleasure, or euphoria. The more endorphin receptors a person has inherited, the better able they are to tolerate pain. Endorphins are triggered immediately in the event of serious injury, broken bones, or severe internal trauma to mask the pain for a short time while you distance yourself from further injury or threat, improving your chance of survival. The first synthetic opioid became available to treat chronic and acute pain in the early 1800s. Fast forward to the present day. The use of diverse forms of that drug to manage physical and emotional pain for legitimate reasons, as well as illegal use in an attempt to sustain feelings of euphoria, have spiraled out of all control. In a report issued by the United Nations Office of

Drugs and Crime, dated June 2020, globally "over 269 million people used drugs in 2018... representing an 30% increase in 10 years... while 35.6 million suffer from drug use disorders." Pre-pandemic, in the US, death from opioids, including prescriptions and illicit drugs, had escalated to over 69,000 per year. According to the CDC (Centers for Disease Control and Prevention), drug overdose is now the leading cause of accidental death in the United States.

Fortunately, researchers in the field of biomedical science have discovered simple, more accessible, and healthier ways to initiate release of endorphins including walking, running, dancing, and sniffing vanilla or lavender. And, leaving the best for last, most of us have at some point reached for a bar of dark chocolate when we've been a little blue; it's the most delicious way to a quick endorphin fix. Tried and true.

Though typically recognized as a brain chemical, most of the neurotransmitter serotonin is produced in the digestive tract. It exerts a dynamic influence over appetite and digestion, mood balance, sleep patterns, self-esteem, and social behavior. Researchers have found one of the most significant factors influencing the flow of serotonin in the brain is the perception of social status. Others' perception of us matters, although even that is a matter of interpretation. You may have an experience of being rejected, excluded for reasons wholly unrelated to who you are. With an increase in our perceived status, acceptance, and acknowledgment, we experience a corresponding increase in serotonin levels, and when we experience a loss of status, serotonin levels drop. The same occurs anytime we receive negative feedback from people we care about or whose opinion of us matters, or when we experience defeat or are criticized or rejected. Therein lies the dark side of excessive social media use. Among the negative consequences of too much online status seeking, studies of college students have found that the more time spent on social media, the more likely they are to have lower grades and poor study habits. Researchers from Harvard Medical School concluded that "social habits are more important than diet and exercise" in the maintenance of long-term overall health.

When we feel good, and serotonin levels are normal or higher, we are relaxed, confident, optimistic, cooperative, sociable, and emotionally stable. Depletion of this hormone is attributed, in the main, to chronic stress and multitasking. Lowered levels across younger and adult populations have been shown to cause cravings for carbohydrate and sugar-laden food, low energy, depression, disrupted sleep, difficulty making decisions, anxiety disorders, and obesity. Weight gain and obesity are linked to disturbed sleep patterns, which interfere with the production of *leptin*, the hormone which decreases appetite, and *ghrelin*, which stimulates appetite, increases food intake, and promotes fat storage.

If you identify with any of these symptoms, you might also consider increasing your intake of specific foods such as slow-release complex carbohydrates including brown rice, pasta, and whole grains, which help maintain your energy levels and boost serotonin. Other foods to consider that help your body produce more serotonin contain tryptophan, an essential amino acid. These include eggs, salmon, turkey, meat, cottage cheese, and pumpkin and sesame seeds.

Often referred to as the love hormone, *Oxytocin* plays a major role in bonding and social functions, the female reproductive process, childbirth, and breastfeeding for both mother and child. Its levels are boosted during sex and orgasm and are evident in high levels in both partners within the first six to nine months of a new relationship. Remember that euphoric feeling of "floating on cloud nine" when you were in love? That was your oxytocin in full flight.

As humans, we are intuitively driven to seek connection, friendship, intimacy, safety, and social trust, which can be reinforced by the simple act of touch and physical proximity. In our formative years, feelings of acceptance, security, and safety are for the most part provided from within our birth family. Later, that role may be filled within a supportive work environment, memberships in social or sporting clubs, inclusion within spiritual or religious communities, or by sharing other common interests. People who live in isolation, feel lonely or ostracized, have few friendships, or are unable to relate well to others are shown to have lower levels of oxytocin.

Some of the most extreme and disturbing examples of this type of emotional deprivation have been found in children who have become orphaned or abandoned by parents living in poverty and consequently institutionalized. International studies conducted by researchers in the fields of child growth and development have revealed that infants and children in some overseas facilities are typically not held or touched. They can be left isolated for prolonged periods and deprived of other sensory or cognitive stimulation by caregivers who are either poorly trained or insensitive to their needs. In the majority of cases, their lives are governed by strict adherence to institutional routines. Overall, these children were found to have low levels of oxytocin and vasopressin, which regulate anxiety, depression, and social behavior. Long-term effects include compromised physical growth, brain development, and language, cognition, and social-emotional development. Specific behavioral difficulties related to this include inattention, overactivity, anger management, aggression, and attachment disorders. The potential for recovery varies depending upon the age at which a child is institutionalized, how long they live within the environment, and the degree of deprivation to which they are exposed.

Even slight changes to your lifestyle can elevate oxytocin levels. Most important is to increase your opportunities for social contact (other than online) and spend real time with friends and family you trust – people with whom you can be yourself. Some people just bring you down, so avoid spending time with anyone who makes you feel uncomfortable or unsupported. Join a meet-up group to make new connections, and when you do, be selective and patient in the process of developing mutual respect and trust. Also, be trustworthy yourself and don't betray confidences. Have a regular massage or go online to find soothing self-massage techniques – such as Qi Gong, which relieves stress, as does acupuncture. Meditate, practice yoga, sing or listen to music, eat healthy food, or play with your pet.

YOUR STRESS HORMONES – A REALITY CHECK

Chronic stress has become our new normal. We think it can be dealt with effectively by a daily detour to "Doctor Starbucks" or by reaching for a chocolate-iced doughnut. In reality, it's the cause of physical illness and emotional dysfunction associated with adrenal fatigue and a compromised immune system. Setting aside the overwhelming and devastating impact of the pandemic on our mental as well as physical health, the challenges of present-day life are seemingly endless. We are constantly challenged by multitasking, inadequate nutrition, interpersonal conflict, tight work deadlines, managing our children's schedules, financial pressures, blended family factions, illness or the death of a loved one, divorce or separation, and/or exposure to environmental toxins – not to mention the disturbing influence of the media. We think we are coping…until we're not.

Our bodies are physiologically adaptive to *irregular bursts* of acute stress, whether real –such as a physical threat of an approaching cyclone or fire – or a psychological threat, which manifests as anxiety. Common examples are the anxiety associated with public speaking, fear of job loss, and social phobias such as fear of eating in public or fear of flying. In those circumstances, the adrenal glands trigger the release of the stress hormones: *adrenaline, cortisol,* and *norepinephrine*. Among other responses, they provide a surge of energy that prepares us to cope and confront or allows us to distance ourselves from the expectation of pain or other unwelcome consequence. We know that as the "fight or flight response". Our energy is drawn away from non-essential functions such as digestion and immunity and diverted to emergency functions, allowing more oxygen into the lungs, increasing blood flow and glucose levels in the muscles, and dilating the pupils to take in as much light as possible. If the threat is physical, when the crisis is over, the body can take from twenty minutes to an hour to relax so that functions return to normal. For some people, it takes two or three days.

In contrast, when a crisis or chronic stress is caused by a psychological or emotional challenge, the body is unable to return to a complete state of relaxation and homeostasis because the issue is unresolved and remains on your mind. In a crisis situation, cortisol production is in overdrive; it is designed to protect you, help you cope. However, when stress levels remain heightened over longer periods, the capacity of your nervous system and adrenal glands to support your needs adequately is compromised, and ultimately cortisol production comes to a halt. As a result, permanent physiological changes occur as adrenal fatigue impairs your ability to function normally.

If you have been feeling overwhelmed and not at your best for a while, be on the lookout for these common symptoms:

- Extreme fatigue throughout the day
- Disrupted sleep patterns, which are associated with weight gain/abdominal fat
- Food cravings – particularly for carbohydrates, salty, or sweet foods
- Difficulty getting up in the morning
- Inability to handle stress
- Addiction to caffeine
- Brain fog
- Depression
- Low sex drive
- Impaired digestion
- Loss of muscle mass

Although adrenal fatigue is not yet recognized by endocrinologists and most allopathic doctors as an illness or disease, many of those same medicos agree that the symptoms are predominantly stress related and could be the precursor of other, more life-threatening conditions. The good news is that in its early stages, adrenal fatigue is reversible and much easier to do than you might think.

TIPS FOR A HEALTHIER, HAPPIER LIFESTYLE

Restoring your vitality requires that you take better care of yourself. That might look like a change in dietary habits to include the right balance of proteins, life-saving greens, and healthy fats; boosting your nutrition with specific natural supplements; or increasing vitamin D levels particularly through fall and winter. Other options that have both short and long-term beneficial effects include: a switch to decaffeinated teas and coffee; spending time outdoors; adopting better sleep habits – such as detaching from all electronic devices at least an hour before bed; and regular practice of meditation and/or yoga. Last, but certainly not the least important, is learning when to say NO.

For years before my confrontation with cancer, I suffered through long bouts of depression; chronic digestive issues, including IBS and celiac disease (undiagnosed till much later); under-active thyroid; constant craving for pastries and pasta; severe allergic reactions to a range of foods I'd eaten since childhood; and irregular sleep patterns. Coping with a stressful job, relationship issues, and those physical challenges every day depleted my reserves. Burnt out, but pressing on regardless as a determined Type A personality, I couldn't remember what it felt like to be relaxed, happy, and healthy.

With no idea that the collective symptoms were indicative of adrenal exhaustion, my approach to recovering my health was piecemeal. One of the first steps I took towards a healthier diet was to switch my daily cup, or two, of strong espresso coffee for a variety of herbal teas. Easier said than done, but I achieved it nevertheless and now very much enjoy herbal teas. I figured if I felt calmer, less frenetic, it would be easier to make other more ambitious changes.

Seeking the advice of a naturopathic doctor, a herbalist, and a psychotherapist gave me the structure and direction I needed. And yet, for all the optimism, concerted effort, and good intention, I often lost momentum. I gave into cravings for those yummy pastries, which by the way were not gluten-free; had way too much Merlot too often to drown my sorrows; and lapsed into other familiar self-sabotaging attitudes and behaviors. Even though I made meaningful progress, it was frustrating that I was unable to sustain it for more than a few weeks at a time.

What I hadn't understood was that sustainable change could only happen when I had rid myself of the self-sabotaging beliefs and low self-esteem that kept me stuck in that repetitive cycle. Now choices, decisions, and change come easy. I listen to my body, and I am happy, healthy, and more mindful. You can be, too.

You have an awesome amount of creative energy at your disposal! Along with your body's unique capacity to rebound, your brilliant brain is a priceless gift, beyond measure. Starting now, please give it more love. It will help you heal the damage already done, create a radical perspective of your future, and bring you joy – but only when you surrender to its power. Following is a summary of Key Concepts for your review. As you move forward to the next chapter, accept that you are no longer a victim or a passive observer, but profoundly instrumental in the creation of your life's path.

BIOGRAPHY BECOMES BIOLOGY

- 98% of human DNA is epigenome sequences that act as control switches to either activate or deactivate gene function.
- Those control switches are triggered by emotions, beliefs, and environmental factors relayed to the brain as electrical impulses.
- Electrical impulses (messages) transmit at speeds up to 270 miles per hour – that's quicker than a blink of an eye. Awesome!
- Over your lifetime, billions of neurons and trillions of synapses are created or strengthened when you develop a new life-affirming habit.
- Positive changes in anatomy and behavior follow as your endocrine system releases happy hormones that reinforce well-being.
- Your brain responds equally to an imagined event as it does to a lived experience. Who knew?
- 95% of life activity has its foundation in the subconscious.
- Reprogramming of emotions and beliefs can only happen when you are in harmony with your subconscious.
- Constructive use of your imagination in the role of observer acts as the catalyst of change.

tips, tools, and techniques

*"Your work is to discover your world,
and then with all of your heart, give yourself to it."*

Buddha

Chapter 5

Discovering Your World

The mind-body-spirit connection is an intricate puzzle of beliefs, misconceptions, emotions, and aspirations, all of which are merely forms of interactive energy that define your quality of life. Sometimes it feels like those elements are connected by a network of gossamer-fine threads; other times like they are clamped as firmly as a limpet to a rock. That intricate relationship may sound complex, but it's not when broken down into its constituent parts. This chapter will help you to gain a perspective on how you came to be you. You will also learn how the simple practice of setting daily intentions to initiate and reinforce positive pathways in your brain can change the color of your world and of your future. That understanding is empowering and freeing. It means your life no longer needs to be defined by fears and past misjudgments. You do not have to feel hopeless or helpless in any way, nor ever feel like a victim.

Standing in the way of your life goals and sustainable happiness is your past – guilt, fear, regrets, suffering, mistakes, shame, and so on. More accurately, it is the way in which you have, or have not, processed life events that has left an indelible impression on your emotions and undermined your ideals, hopes, and dreams.

Studies have revealed that your personality – the distinctive way you learn about and interpret the world, and your behaviors and attitudes – usually is developed by age seven. It is influenced in part by your genetic predisposition (your temperament) and in major part by your environment, specifically by the quality of parenting from infancy. Parents who are engaged and sensitive learn about their child's adaptive response to certain situations and are better able to prepare them to overcome those and potentially more difficult challenges in the future. In the best-case scenario, parents provide loving care and a stable, predictable environment so that children learn who to respect and trust, and the family evolves as a cohesive, supportive unit through to adulthood. In contrast are those children and adults whose maladaptive behaviors range from the quirkily absurd and amusing through to the delinquent, deviant, and criminal as regularly featured in our daily newsfeeds. The theory that their behaviors are the result of ineffective parenting continues to be a contentious issue among social scientists.

Regardless of who is to blame and for what, we have already learned from the new science of epigenetics that your inheritance extends far beyond your genetic makeup. It is highly likely you will enter your teen years plagued by the same fears, anxieties, misconceptions, and behaviors as your parents. Then, as you venture into the external world – subject to offerings from our education and legal systems, society and local culture, and blitzes every hour of the day by advertisers, news reports, or fake facts – you are subtly taught who and what to believe. This process of socialization is crucial to our development as an individual Self.

As we become exposed to contrasts in parenting styles and family dynamics, explore cross-cultural boundaries, develop social and intimate relationships, and learn new skills, our Self becomes more well defined. Newfound values often conflict with those of our parents. We intuitively seek connection with like-minded, relatable others who have the potential to provide acceptance, appreciation, friendship, and support. That community may be a workplace; a group sharing political, sporting, business, or spiritual interests; or a subculture such as birdwatchers, bikers, body-builders, fashionistas, Francophiles, LGBTQ+ (lesbian, gay, bisexual, transgender and associated communities), or video gamers. Being understood, accepted, and respected within your chosen community reinforces your self-image, elevates your social status, boosts your self-esteem, gives your life meaning, and provides the opportunity to build valuable relationships. You belong. You feel excited and grateful to be there; your reward-oriented (dopamine) and bonding-oriented (oxytocin) hormones are surging.

However, if you succumb to the status-quo without resistance or at least curiosity to explore an alternative reality, you place yourself at risk of becoming a Conditioned Self. Gradually, your True Self becomes barely recognizable, banished to the deepest recesses of your cellular memory. Over time, as a Conditioned Self, you routinely yield to unspoken peer pressure to become part of the collective consciousness – the tribe mentality that conforms and avoids disagreement. You feel safe and comfortable within the tribe. You would do just about anything to protect your social stature, despite the awareness that you are at risk of living as a victim when you consistently allow others to make decisions for you. If you resist the persistent urge to be independent, you undermine any chance you ever had to realize your dreams or reach your full potential. I assure you that once that profound sense of dissatisfaction and of being stifled nestles into your bones, it's not going anywhere soon. Your True Self is knocking, determined to be heard.

It takes courage to venture away from the tribe and find a different way forward. We worry what that might look like and who we would be without it. We are immobilized by the fear of social alienation, criticism, loneliness, judgment, or rejection by the people we know and love, even when our circumstances become unbearable. Overwhelmed, we forget we have been born with the innate capacity to adapt and to respond instinctively to our environment with creativity, optimism, and determination.

You know with every fiber of your being that it's time to move on but can't seem to find a way out, a starting point. Your resistance is grounded in a mess of conflicting emotions, past events, happy and painful memories. Cast your mind back to the best-ever birthday present you received as a child or in your teens, or the best-ever fun event. Like most of us, you will be able to describe it in vivid detail. You remember where you were and whether it was summer, winter, or spring, that bright blue dress or new sport jacket, your first pair of party-shoes or Nike sneakers, your first date, or what you and your partner wore to the prom. Decades later, they still bring a smile because attached to your recall are warm feelings of fun, freedom, positive self-esteem, and being valued. Buried deep within your subconscious, they have no doubt shaped your beliefs and attitudes towards child-rearing years later.

Painful memories are processed in the same way. Over long or chronic periods of distress or unwanted upheaval, collective traumas and self-defeating beliefs take front and center stage and cause happy times, hope, courage, and resilience to fade into the background. You wake up every day feeling defeated, wounded, victimized, and helpless. That is until today, as you remember you have a solution right here in your hands.

SETTING CONSCIOUS INTENTION – THE FIRST STEP TO A MINDFUL EXISTENCE

Conscious intention captures our dreams, imagination, and aspirations. When infused with life-affirming emotion, it has the power to change your life. I discovered in the early stages of developing the program that has now become this book, that addressing either element independently in the hope of creating sustainable change is futile. Imagine life as a black-and-white movie nuanced by shades of grey. It features an intelligent plot, a comfortable yet far-from-perfect setting, a charismatic lead role, interesting characters in support roles, ongoing challenges for the hero/heroine to overcome, and of course romance. While it may have substance, sharply defined edges, and entertainment value, its tone is muted and uninspiring. Contrast that level of audience engagement with the same film in color. Color brings it to life, creates a radiantly illuminated environment, adds complexity and depth, enhances the inherent beauty of the geographic, social, and cultural contexts, adds sensuality, and reels us in to connect at a deeper level. In the same way, positive emotion brings conscious intention to life.

That reality first became evident as I attempted to untangle the many complex causes of my chronic depression and subsequent cancer. Believing that the only way to survive was to be tough and resilient and that any show of emotion was a sign of weakness, I lived in my head. For decades, I suppressed emotional expression in an effort to stop the floodgates from opening and to avoid a complete breakdown. I had one anyway. Funny how that works. Later, I was to hear the same story from many others, both *left-brain thinkers* – logical, analytical, and objective – and *right-brain thinkers* or *creatives* – intuitive, imaginative, and passionate. Working through the healing scripts with the left-brain thinkers, we made noticeable but slower progress. Though clear and specific in their intention and beliefs, they found it difficult to acknowledge the relevance of their emotional history. In later sessions, and in all other cases of clients readily acknowledging their emotional burdens, results were more immediate, profound, and lasting.

We discovered in Chapter 3 that 70% of people's thoughts are negative or redundant. And we know from psychologists and other mental health practitioners that most unhappy people are plagued with fear and doubt. Those are both strong motivating influences, keeping us from our goals and eroding our capacities to be creative, enthusiastic, and productive. The tools and tips in this segment of the book teach you how to reverse those statistics. They empower you to create new positive neural pathways that reinforce optimism, creativity, curiosity, resilience, gratitude, kindness, compassion, imagination, excitement, spontaneity, inspiration, and hope.

One of the simplest, most powerful demonstrations of how *conscious intention can alter physical reality* was provided by Dr. Masaru Emoto, a Japanese researcher and a doctor of alternative medicine. His experiments, documented in his book, *Messages from Water*, became popular in the first decade of the new millennium, following their inclusion in the documentary *What the Bleep Do We Know!?*, which attempted to explain quantum theory to a broader, non-scientific audience. Dr. Emoto established that conscious thought and language, specifically the terms *love* and *gratitude,* changed the molecular structure and appearance of water crystals.

For the experiments, water samples were taken from twice-distilled hospital-quality water sources. Approximately 2,000 people in Tokyo were instructed to send positive intention towards samples located in an electromagnetically sealed room in California. Control samples were also set aside in various other locations. In response to positive language, music, and prayer, the molecular structure of the original untreated samples was, in all cases, transformed into a variety of beautiful, complex ice crystal formations. Other samples exposed to negative influences manifested the opposite results. All results were blindly identified and photographed by independent judges, and the photographic evidence of change included in his publication.

You might be wondering what that has to do with you and your own creative capacity. Water is the major component in most body parts; in fact, the average adult is comprised of over 60% water. It is critical for the effective functioning of the brain; plays a key role in digestion, assimilation, and elimination; lubricates the joints; acts as a shock absorber for the brain and spinal cord; regulates body temperature; and facilitates cellular growth, reproduction, and survival. You would die without it. Setting aside what you have learned about happy hormones, neurotransmitters, negative thought patterns, external epigenetic influences, organ transplants, and neuroplasticity, now you have another constructive concept to consider. That is, more scientific proof that over 60% of you is reprogrammable and immediately responsive to positive intentions and words.

Dr. Emoto went on to conduct a similar, equally famous experiment, which you might find interesting. Using cooked rice placed in two separate containers, he instructed school children to read the label on each container out loud for thirty days. On one container were the words "thank you", and on the other were "you fool". After the test period, the rice in the container with the words "you fool" had become moldy and rotten. The rice in the other container was relatively unchanged. Many of my clients and students have conducted the same experiments with rice and reported similar results.

Every morning before I get out of bed, with my eyes closed, I set my daily intention before I'm distracted by practicalities. I repeat it once or twice, then sit in silence and stillness while it settles into my bones. Over the years, I've learned a bit about conscious intention as it relates to the quantum field of infinite potential.

At first, while I got it that we are all floating around in this infinite stream of possibility, I didn't understand the need to be specific about my aspirations and what I intended to happen. Also, I learned that the vibration associated with "begging" for something to happen, out of sheer desperation, was not the way to approach it either. When we beg or plead, we come from a place of neediness, are driven by a sense of lack, and feel out of control. Those feelings are typically underpinned by doubt and fear: doubt that you will ever get what you want, doubt that you deserve it, doubt that there is any such field of potential. When you are no longer shackled by those misconceptions and corrosives emotions, your hopes and dreams are more easily attainable because you radiate a more optimistic and expectant vibration. This allows transformation to unfold with ease and grace, aligned with the natural order of things.

The good news is that you don't have to worry about it once you have surrendered your intention to the Universe. Your True Self knows and trusts that everything will happen in its own time. No need to know the details, either. From experience, I can tell you that often the solution, resource, or answer you are seeking manifests in quite a different way than how you expected. Now, *I love not knowing*. The uncertainty is exciting! Overcoming the need (in truth it was almost an obsession) to be in charge of the how, when, and where was one of my biggest hurdles. So glad I did.

EXERCISE: SCRIPT FOR SETTING CONSCIOUS INTENTION

As you prepare to set your conscious intention, remember:

- Intentions are always set in the present moment, not in the future. Include the words "am now", as opposed to "will be". Grab the goal or intention from out there and bring it right in to your present-day reality, regardless of what that might be.
- Believe in your own power and trust you are in partnership with the flow of All That Is.

Now begin with a script to set your intention. You can use the one that follows or adapt it to what feels comfortable for you.

SETTING CONSCIOUS INTENTION

As co-creator of my Best Life, I draw upon the stream of limitless potential, love, compassion, and wisdom. I am that which I aspire to be.

Next introduce the variable. It might be as simple as: "I am creative, resourceful, and optimistic," or whatever else you aspire to in the moment. Sometimes, you may find there is no need to say anything else. Simply relax and allow images or feelings to arise unforced.

I always face the day feeling optimistic, and I wish the same for you in the very near future. These exercises are the first step.

TAKING CONTROL OF YOUR FUTURE. SIMPLY. SAFELY.

Are you worried that the exercises are too hard or convoluted, or that you will be unable to do them for other reasons? If you are, you're wrong on both counts. Children have done them with remarkable results. They treat it like a game and go wild with their imagination. Following are a few observations from people I've worked with using these protocols. Be excited, read on.

NOTE: Since I began gathering testimonials, endorsements, and quality-assurance feedback from my life-coaching/psychotherapy practice, I have guaranteed clients and workshop participants absolute anonymity. It encouraged them to speak freely. So, you will find no actual names (except Dr. Marc Boutet, ND) attached to the following testimonials, although I assure you that each is authentic. The same applies to client case studies throughout the book. All names and identifiers have been altered. Many more, from health practitioners and clients can be found on my website.

Deanna's program is an impressively effective therapy on the mind/body level. A safe way to disconnect the emotional component from memories, release destructive thought patterns, and move forward as a freer more authentic you. I would challenge anyone to try this therapy and not get meaningful results. (Dr. Marc Boutet, ND, BC, Canada)

What differentiates your work from the many others I have been to is the immediacy of the results. I can't believe these issues, most of which I've had for over twenty years, have been released. But I know they are, I am changed. (Darius)

After a few sessions with Deanna, I noticed significant inner changes as limiting beliefs and patterns were released. Painful and challenging relationships were resolved, creating space for more happiness, lightness, and improved self-esteem. I have been able to create better boundaries in my relationships and value myself more. Deanna's grounded and non-judgmental approach created a sense of openness and safety in working with her and allowed for deeper revelations and insights to surface. (Meiling)

My son has always been very sensitive emotionally... would just feel overwhelmed (at school) with all the noise and social demands... his phobias were also getting worse. Deanna met with my son just before Christmas, and he really enjoyed the visit. Within the first week after his first session, I began to see subtle changes. He was more expressive, more assertive, laughing and chatting more... his teacher remarked on his growing confidence... he was even contributing to class discussions. To my amazement, he even started enjoying field trips and parties, which up until then he had always avoided. His reading has improved; he is now happy to try new things. Deanna produced instant results with minimal effort from my son, and I am happy to say I have not seen any of his emotions or behaviors slip back. He is going from strength to strength. I highly recommend Deanna to anyone. She has made a huge difference to my son's life. The results are really quite incredible. I still can't quite believe it. Thank you. (Jodie)

After suffering from bulimia for over twenty years, I have been 100% healed within five sessions of working with Deanna. Thank you for giving me my birthright back. I am now living with peace and joy every day. (Kristina)

My takeaway message was one of possibility, positive regard, and knowing that in any instance or thought, I am able to heal, transform, or shift. I am grateful for the remarkable example of boundaries and balance Deanna demonstrates. This modeling will facilitate me in my personal and professional roles. (Allison)

There are no words to express the gratitude for all you have done to help, support, and guide my family! I am a different person today because of you. You not only helped me on my healing path (and continue to do so) but provided me with the tools to help others. All my life I have "talk counselled" others, but now I have these incredible tools and gifts to help others on a completely different energy level. (Destiny)

Thank you... it is still a wonderment to me that something so easy can have such a powerful effect in changing our lives. (Enid)

I really appreciate your insights and support. Just to let you know I have generally felt lighter, more relaxed inside myself, and have more energy. I am not running an inner background dialogue of self-judgment – "shoulds", etc. I have more interest to connect with people, although I also recognize the need to take it easy. (Marie)

Over the past twelve years, I have tried a wide variety of healing techniques. In all those modalities, I have not encountered another approach to healing that yields such positive results for my mind, body, and spirit in such a short period, and with so little angst associated with the process. Thank you for the positive outcomes you have helped me to create to heal my family relationships, for my business venture that has tripled in revenue during the time that we have worked together, and for your help to heal from a long-standing back injury. What you do is magical. (Tessa)

Thank you for the help you have given me over the course of our sessions. You have demonstrated an ability to see through the myriad symptoms and outward manifestations of my perceived dis-ease to the core of my true self. In this process, I have discovered that I am and always have been an integral and irreplaceable part of the divine plan. I am now more able to live with integrity and hope and to offer my gifts to the world with true generosity. (Sven)

Since my sessions with Deanna, all done remotely through Skype, this personal search has shifted to sorting, clarity, and healing. I have a more open, accepting, and compassionate perspective of myself, life, and spiritual matters. I also feel less complicated and emotionally lighter. Most of all, I have never felt so valuable and empowered. (Jasmine)

Chapter 6

Accessing Your Creative Genius

It's time to turn your focus deeper inward. This chapter includes tips, simple preparatory exercises, and client case studies to help you make the best of your intentions and a powerful connection to your creative intelligence.

Their power lies in their *simplicity*, so you may initially find yourself questioning their ability to be effective. I'd like a dollar for every time someone has raised that question and been astounded by the immediacy of the results. Those questions inevitably arise from a cluttered mind.

Culturally, we tend towards multitasking to get things done. We start each day on automatic pilot; our focus primarily centered around organizing and planning how much we can pack into an average day or week. That habit creates compounding levels of stress and disconnectedness, which compromise our ability to live in a state of higher consciousness. Most of us think we are good at multitasking, but multiple studies have proven us wrong. Instead, they show that taking one task at a time and completing it before moving on can increase your productivity by up to 40%. Who wouldn't want that? From a paper published in the *World Psychiatry* journal, we learn that "digital distractions" are changing the way our brains work – not always in a good way. Children are experiencing "decreased verbal intelligence", and among adults, there is now a tendency towards "cognitive offloading", meaning we no longer bother to remember what we can find online. Nor should it come as a surprise that attention spans have also declined. Results of a study conducted by Microsoft Corporation found the attention span of device users (which is almost everyone in the developed world) has dropped significantly since the year 2000, when it was on average twelve seconds. It is now eight seconds on average – "less than that of a goldfish, which has a span of nine seconds." Don't be a goldfish.

At this moment, you are laying the foundations of an entirely new and exciting future. The significance of this program is immeasurable; it has changed lives for the better in unimaginable ways. Here's the thing: in order to work, it needs your full attention and creative input. Would you prepare for your university entrance exams by partying every night, with hordes of people coming and going, endless chatter, music blaring from Bose wall-to-wall speakers, sipping red wine or guzzling beer, munching on Doritos and salsa dip, while constantly checking your cell phone for fear of missing out? I don't think so. Stay focused.

Think often and optimistically on your intentions and aspirations. Keeping them at the forefront of your mind will discourage negative and self-sabotaging thoughts. Every decision you make from this day forward needs to encompass them and contribute to your forward momentum. That is the turning point, the foundation of your new reality, as it was mine. There isn't a day in my life that I don't acknowledge spirituality as my highest value; it governs everything I do. I'm not suggesting that it needs to be *your* highest value. But that acknowledgment led me from a rigid workaholic existence to where I am right now, living an interesting, productive, and joyful life. Be deliberate in your thoughts, words, and actions every day. To help you stay engaged, here is another of my all-time favorite quotes: "The secret of change is to focus all of your energy, not on the old, but on building the new." *Socrates*

ACHIEVING THE BEST OUTCOMES

These guidelines are designed to shift your focus away from conscious awareness of the distractions and clutter surrounding you and towards a connection to your subconscious and a quieter mind. *Your intention has to be deep-seated within the subconscious for your creative efforts to take hold.* When you are in that zone, transitions from old ways of thinking happen in the blink of an eye. In approaching any of the exercises:

- Be patient and kind to yourself. Most important is that you be consistent. Your neural pathways have been reinforcing the things you *don't* want for years: worries about finances, poor self-image, relationship issues, your health, children, politics, and on it goes. Stop letting them control your life now.
- Trust that your efforts are supported by the Universe or God, The One, All That Is, Divine Intelligence, Source, Universal Mind, or other Deity of your choosing. If you prefer a scientific approach, quantum refers to this phenomenon as "the

field of infinite potential", wherein all things are possible and accessible. Whatever you acknowledge as the Ultimate Source of Creation will work for you when you surrender to it.
- Relax. Be willing to shift to a more fluid state of creativity, expression, and spontaneity, where you allow change to happen organically rather than attempting to construct an outcome. Let go of the need to control. Just *being* invites connection and awareness; *doing* creates distraction.
- Caffeine. You will not be surprised, I'm sure, to learn that for most people, having a few shots of coffee just before sitting down to these exercises will be counterproductive. The aim is to have you feeling calm, Zen-like.
- The proven power of the exercises alongside the "weeding and seeding" scripts lie in their simplicity. Honor it.
- Fundamental to your success is the willingness to use your imagination creatively. Quantum physics teaches that thoughts are just another form of energy present as either particles or waves – dependent only upon whether they are being observed. Your role will be the Observer. Your subconscious responds instantly because it doesn't distinguish between a real-time or a virtual experience.
- During the release, when you close your eyes to become the Observer, allow your body's response to unfold through to completion without rushing before opening your eyes.
- Stay in the moment; be present. It will be so much easier to identify and rid yourself of corrosive emotions and unwanted habits and then move on to seed life-affirming options.
- Be confident in your innate abilities. Follow the guidelines to the letter, as prescribed. They work. After just a short while,

the scripts become second nature. Fear, doubt, and disbelief are the only blocks to your success.

You may already have the knack of being able to relax at will, detach from your conscious awareness, and allow the quiet to wash over you. If so, kudos to you. That part of the process, preparing for what is to come, can be challenging for many people. But that is about as challenging as it gets; the rest is quite simple. No need to rush or compare yourself to others, either. What matters is consistency, not pace.

As you allow your body and mind to relax as the Observer, constructive images or happy feelings arise unforced from your subconscious to support your transition. These stem from your unique life experience, imagination, and motivations. Sometimes they will take on a different form than other times, perhaps more vivid or intense, other times less so.

CASE NOTES   **MEET STEPHANIE: THE OBSERVER**

Stephanie loves to cycle on the weekend with a mixed group of forty-somethings. They ride for hours, then stop for a hearty brunch and caffeine. These get-togethers are a meaningful part of her life. When wanting to replace any outdated habits, thoughts, or emotions with a new choice, her mind typically wanders to what will make her happiest. She starts the transition by visualizing herself at home feeling gloomy and lazy, then sees herself on a virtual shopping trip downtown looking for bright, new cycling shorts and a jersey until she finds the perfect look. When she does, she feels instantly energized and radiant – her blue mood has lifted. Lastly, she sees herself heading towards home feeling refreshed, optimistic, and happy. The negative beliefs or emotions no longer resonate, and fresh creative concepts emerge in their place. A surge in her levels of dopamine and serotonin have saved the day.

Another client loves to cook and sees himself as an amateur chef, so his transitional process often involves shopping for the perfect food through to the creation of a delicious meal shared with friends.

If you are inclined more towards feeling experiences rather than visualizing them, that works just as well. Observe the feelings. You might start feeling heavy, unhappy, stuck, or even have some emotional or physical discomfort in some part of your body. As you sit in stillness in your role of Observer, you will gradually experience feelings of lightness and of being energized, freer, more relaxed, and happier.

Back in the day, when I was a control-freak running on adrenaline, sitting still for any amount of time was a challenge, unless I was watching a movie or reading. I just couldn't relax. With practice and sheer determination, I learned to sit in stillness, allowing the process to happen spontaneously. I still remember the first transition over which I surrendered complete control. Initially, a solid six-foot-high red-brick wall presented itself, without any prompting from me. It just sat there staring back at me for a bit. Then came stage two: a few previously undamaged random bricks crumbled and vanished into thin air. Suddenly from left field, their bright, shining, solid gold substitutes flew into place. I got the message. Funny and awesome.

Most of us power through the day with no conscious awareness of how we feel at any given moment unless we are confronted with a crisis. We are so busy focusing externally that we don't allow our true thoughts and emotions to surface. Or, if we do notice them, we intentionally set them aside to be dealt with later, much later – which often means not at all, because something else comes up that is more urgent or less stressful. Just like an ostrich, we bury our head in the sand, hoping it will all just go away. And, if you are brought up to be polite and accommodating, or to be seen and not heard, as I was, you will tend to suppress just about every thought and emotion that has the potential to cause embarrassment or unpleasant consequences for either yourself or others. That was your old life.

CASE NOTES **MEET JESSICA: THE OSTRICH**

Jessica was a thirty-six-year-old mom who doted on her two boys and was actively involved in their activities. Aspiring to be the best-ever mom, or at least a vast improvement on her own experiences as a kid, she attended all the parent-teacher conferences, made sure that homework assignments were submitted on time, contributed to fundraising activities, gave the kids a healthy breakfast every morning, and had a regular evening routine that would ensure them a restful night's sleep. She had met most of her girlfriends through her children's school years ago when the children had the same classes and sporting commitments. Always first to raise her hand when help was needed, she collected other kids to take to or from school, participated in the local mothers' support groups, joined her husband in the bleachers to cheer on the baseball team, and usually baked cookies or muffins for morning tea following Sunday morning church services. She was almost always the designated driver on social occasions. She liked to be popular, the one her friends knew they could always rely on.

Somehow, over a year ago, she had been persuaded by a few of the more self-indulgent girlfriends in her friendship circle to do the monthly Costco run. That involved taking everyone's orders, which would often change at a moment's notice, driving the almost twenty-mile round trip at her own expense, shopping, then standing in line sometimes for too long, and sorting it all at home for them to collect. Her efforts were now taken for granted with little thanks or compensation. Jessica's stress levels escalated out of control when she finally realized she was being manipulated. She felt betrayed and disrespected, not for the first time, by people she thought were her friends. That realization was the straw that broke the camel's back. There she was in my office sobbing, confused, seething with resentment, and looking for a solution.

As we talked, she admitted that she rarely said "no," because "it's not the right thing to do." And, for the same reason, she repressed her *true* feelings about a few of the group who were demeaning. When overlooked, or more overtly mistreated, she chose to be an ostrich and bury her head in the sand, not wanting to put those relationships at risk or to be seen as needy. She hoped if she didn't acknowledge her feelings, they would go away. We agreed, having revisited similar scenarios, that this pattern of avoidance and repressing her true feelings had been a default position for more years than she cared to remember. In the process, she lost her sense of True Self and her right to express an opinion and to say "no" when it compromised her own well-being.

Ideally, in the creation of your new reality you are emancipated, self-accepting, openly expressive, growth-oriented, spontaneous, loving, compassionate, and not paralyzed by others' opinions. That is your True Self, where you want to be. The problem is that you are no longer sure of what it might feel like to acknowledge the importance of your own feelings or voice your true opinions; it's been so long. You are not alone. You share that tendency with countless others, although the circumstances that give rise to it are not always a matter of choice.

Many of the adults I have worked with suffered an atrocious childhood. Some from war-torn regions being witness to things no child should ever see; others were subject to cruel physical and emotional abuse in so-called civilized environments not far from where I'm sitting, or had been institutionalized or placed in foster-care from an early age, or left abandoned in the street, homeless and hungry. More often, they were from ordinary families, in ordinary neighborhoods, where they experienced deprivation due to parental neglect. What undermined their happiness, what they shared in common, was an inability to connect to important feelings such as hope, pride, self-respect, worthiness, love and tenderness, safety, excitement, optimism, and happiness and joy. Those innate life-affirming emotions govern how we think, what we do, the choices we make, and our interactions with others. Instead, their every thought and action was undermined by deep-seated feelings of hopelessness, confusion, rejection, shame, distrust, and much more. Though severely emotionally handicapped to start, they have transitioned well and since found their happy place.

We started their transition, as we always do, with the following exercises.

EXERCISE: EASY MINDFUL MEDITATION

If you find traditional meditation challenging, this simple version might suit you better. Mindful meditation relieves stress, as it encourages you to gently engage your mind and imagination while drawing it away from external distractions and clutter. It lays the groundwork for the most effective transition. Let's get to it!

- Find a place that is quiet and private, where you are not likely to be interrupted. Allow yourself some me time without the need to hurry.
- Settle into a comfortable chair, allow your body to relax, allow your shoulders to drop, hands in your lap, feet flat on the floor. If you are a meditator and prefer the Lotus position, that's fine too.
- Close your eyes to begin the transition from your external world. Be conscious of your breath coming in through your nose and out from your mouth. Take four or five deep breaths, then go back to regular rhythmic breathing.
- When you are ready, focus your attention on a stream of brilliant crystalline light making its way from the deepest recesses of the cosmos gently towards the top of your head. It represents the source of all Creation, wise, powerful, and resourceful. You sense it descending very slowly, lighting up each cell in your brain, face, ears, and neck. If your attention is drawn to a slight pain behind your eye, or similar distraction, simply observe it and let the light wash over it until it dissolves. Or you might become aware of the tightness in your shoulders

and neck, which you carry every day. Calmly observe it, see the light resting there. It melts away.

- Continue to slowly (read *very* slowly) follow the light down your arms, along your spine, through the organs in your torso, then legs and feet. Address each finger and toe individually. Each time you become aware of any pain or discomfort, linger on that spot until it fades.
- When you are done with your feet and toes, slowly follow the light as it returns to your upper body and settles in your heart. Sit with it there. You may see or feel a surge of emotion or a sense of being so much calmer or happier. Without consciously thinking, you may even have a flash of insight or awareness about something that had previously lacked clarity. Gradually return your attention to the room you are in. Open your eyes.

This type of introspection or meditation, when practiced regularly, has a far-reaching impact on your life. Among other benefits, it promotes clarity of mind and contributes to improved digestive and sleep patterns. On a personal note, it has also heightened my intuition, improved my capacity to focus regardless of whatever is going on around me, and is a prolific source of creative ideas. Let it be for you too. If this was your very first time, and you did not experience a sense of calm, optimism, or well-being, please practice it again *slowly* before moving on to the next exercise.

YOUR SOUL CRAVES FREEDOM OF EXPRESSION

When you practice connecting to your true feelings, you create and reinforce the neural pathways that trigger your happy hormones. Only they have the capacity to change your mindset and mood in an instant. Developing the habit of allowing yourself to feel, rather than think, through your problems, also enhances your faculty of discernment and higher consciousness. Are you one of those people who has allowed that capacity to be dulled or even erased from your routine response patterns due to years of constraint or repression? If so, this exercise has been designed especially for you.

Before my confrontation with cancer, my entire existence was lived mostly within the confines of an over-active left brain, with much less regard for intuitive and feeling capacities. My life revolved around the practicalities of doing, learning, reasoning, and logic, at which I excelled. From an early age, I learned to conceal my emotions, so that no one, particularly my mother, would have the satisfaction of knowing I was hurt or not coping. I became defiant and disconnected, believing it would ensure my survival. On some level that decision proved useful; I'm still here, but in truth, it caused me to be more vulnerable, confused, and dysfunctional and to repeatedly make bad choices.

Initial attempts to understand why I perpetuated self-destructive patterns were scattered. I met with various counselors and spiritual advisors, learned meditation, attended workshops at every opportunity, read so many books, explored numerous religious philosophies, practiced yoga, and whatever else came my way. I was on a fact-finding mission; developing an intellectual understanding of what was fundamentally wrong with me. As time went by, although better informed and armed with an arsenal of self-help tools, I still wasn't happy – nowhere even close to knowing what happy or life-affirming emotions might look like. *How do I get to that place?* I wondered. *And, once I arrive, what will it take to stay there, to wake up every day feeling optimistic, self-assured, and worthy of something better; knowing that I matter?*

Around the time those questions arose, a friend in Brisbane referred me to a psychotherapist who had remarkable results with what she called *emotionally constipated* clients. I more than qualified, and despite being warned of her unconventional methods, remained undeterred. When put to the test, I was unable to reconnect to the everyday emotions I needed to live as a whole person, even though I genuinely wanted to do so. In both conventional and unconventional ways, she presented a range of scenarios that required that I manifest (not merely state) a specific emotional response. I failed. The wall I was hiding behind proved impenetrable during our time together, though I learned much more about functional family dynamics and the roles each member was expected to play. I also no longer blamed myself for what happened in my childhood or for my maladaptive coping mechanisms. Not long after our last session, I suffered a total emotional collapse and was diagnosed with a major depressive disorder and confined to bed for a minimum of three months. It took another twelve months or so for me to transition to a *new normal*, allowing me to be expressive as my True Self. It was freeing.

Our expression of emotion is unquestionably regulated by our cultural norms and values. Western cultures, including American, which promote the development of the Self as *independent* of others, tend towards acceptance of overt expression of emotion; in fact, encourage it. It reinforces the individual's right to be assertive, unique, and in pursuit of competitive goals. In contrast, within societies such as China and Japan, the development of Self occurs primarily within the framework of *interdependent* relationships. Individual goals and motivation take second place to the maintenance of harmonious interpersonal communication, acts of kindness, and open-hearted cooperation. Cooperation is highly valued and believed to enhance resilience, patience, flexibility, and self-control – traits of emotional maturity, while self-assertion is seen as immature and ego driven.

Results from studies in the US and some Western European countries have found the expression of emotional vocabulary in boys and men to be confined to a much narrower spectrum in comparison to girls and women. Biologically, these differences in emotional expression can be attributed to factors such as hormones, which activate emotional arousal systems to a different extent in puberty. From early childhood, girls demonstrate greater language ability and inhibitory control (the ability to suppress or countermand a thought, action, or feeling) than boys. Pre-school peer group playtimes also contribute to the development of stereotypical roles. Boys veer towards the loud, commanding superhero archetype, while girls at play are quieter, more expressive, and cooperative. In our society, men and boys are generally discouraged from expressing emotion from early childhood and are instead told to "man up" for fear of being seen as weak, effeminate, or gay.

Our education system has not always seen the wisdom in addressing the development of emotional intelligence in its curriculum. That aspect of our education is left mostly to ourselves. We get busy with the practicalities of creating a life, exploring food choices, keeping physically fit, acquiring technical skills, finding a job to support our lifestyle, striving for status, experimenting with relationship and community, and planning fabulous vacations to keep stress at bay. Gradually, our natural-born capacity to accept and apply what *we intuitively know and feel, the earliest and truest source of our happiness*, fades into the background.

At heart, what we are all seeking is happiness and well-being. It is a sad comment on the state of the world to admit that happiness has become so elusive its pursuit has become a "thing". It is now the focus of studies across the globe by universities, psychologists, and social scientists. There's even a Happiness Research Institute based in Copenhagen, Denmark and a similar enterprise, the Institute of Happiness based in Gujarat, India, which offers corporate seminars, distance learning, and free counseling. Would you have guessed their research has shown that the accumulation of more "stuff" does not rate too highly as essential to sustaining levels of happiness? Rather, they emphasize:

- The importance of cultivating positive emotions over pure logic
- The role of intuition in decision making.
- The need for meaningful connection

The meteoric rise of Facebook and other social media is proof positive of our intuitive craving for connection, despite those specific types of connection being mostly superficial and incapable of fulfilling the void. Other studies show that experiencing a *broad range* of both positive and negative emotion is crucial to long-term mental health and happiness. They function as signposts to help us define what we need to modify, learn how to respond appropriately, and determine when to process further and what and who to avoid. This next exercise is dedicated to that end.

EXERCISE: CULTIVATING DISCERNMENT

In this exercise, we are looking specifically at *how your body responds* to a statement that is either true or untrue for you. Placing one hand on your solar plexus (several inches above the belly button), with the thumb resting on your sternum is helpful, but not essential, in making the connection.

- Settle into a comfortable chair, allow your body to relax, allow your shoulders to drop, hands in your lap, feet flat on the floor. If you are a meditator and prefer the Lotus position, that's fine too.
- Be conscious of your breath coming in through your nose and out from your mouth. Take four or five deep breaths, then return to regular rhythmic breathing.
- *Slowly* make the following statements, either aloud or to yourself. After saying each one, close your eyes, still with one hand on your solar plexus, and pay attention to your body's response. Wait patiently; it might take a few minutes to become attuned. The more you practice, the more attuned you become.

Use the following examples of **True Statements** for practice:

- My name is…
- I am a man/woman.

- I was born in…
- I have/don't have siblings.
- I have children/no children.
- I am married/not married.
- I am made mostly of water.

Become consciously aware of your body's response. Feel it, don't think it. Usually, statements aligned with your True Self produce feelings of calm, satisfaction, safety, and comfort. Equally, if you are generally at peace, you may remain feeling neutral.

Now use the following examples of **Positive Events and Circumstances** for practice.

- Special place/Favorite fun activity
- Graduation ceremony/Wedding Day
- Award or recognition of excellent performance
- Family gatherings/Birth of children
- First car/First date

Become consciously aware of your body's response. Typically, you will experience an upward surge in your energy levels and an overall sense of well-being. If not, repeat the exercise until you do, before you move on to the next one. Remember those feelings.

It is equally important that you begin to strengthen your intuitive sense of those people and situations that cause discomfort or stress and have the potential to undermine your well-being.

Use the following examples of **False Statements** for practice:

I have intentionally used absurd examples in this segment to exaggerate your experience of how the body intuitively reacts to anything *not* aligned with your True Self. Feel free to use your own, preferably ridiculous or blatantly untrue, examples.

- I am a super cool famous athlete (if you're not)
- I hate reading (if you love it)
- I have red hair and freckles (if you don't)
- I am an astronaut (could be)
- I am a pink hippopotamus living at the zoo (obviously not, they can't read)☺

Become consciously aware of your body's response. Again, feel it, don't think it. Usually, statements *not* aligned with your True Self produce feelings of discomfort like rising anxiety, a surge of emotion, or escalation of muscle tension. It can also manifest as a fleeting pain that has been trapped in some part of your body.

Use the following examples of **Unhappy Circumstances** for practice:

- A major disappointment/betrayal
- An acrimonious divorce/ breakup
- Fractious or difficult relationship at work
- Disharmony at home with spouse, parents, or siblings
- Loss of a loved one; the one you're still pining over, years later
- Financial insecurities

Take your time, perhaps think of more than one example. Allow the response to arise, sit with it, become aware of its physical effects. Allow the emotions, either positive or negative, to arise without succumbing to the urge to avoid them or to stop your practice. Remember those feelings.

So, I want to say: practice, practice, practice expressing how you *really* feel and think with your children, at work, and with friends. Speaking your truth is both freeing and empowering, while the opposite serves only to create confusion, wariness, and frustration. The goal is to develop a more authentic relationship with yourself. It is the key to a happier future.

In the next chapter, we commence a deep-dive into what's keeping you stuck in your current reality – whatever that might be. I'll close this chapter with a thought that has served me well, throughout my life, and in many difficult situations. I wish the same for you.

"Nothing in this world can take the place of persistence. Talent will not; nothing is more common that unsuccessful men with talent. Genius will not; unrewarded genius is almost a proverb. Education will not; the world is full of educated derelicts. Persistence and determination alone are omnipotent. The slogan Press on! Has solved and always will solve the problems of the human race."
Calvin Coolidge

Chapter 7

Emotions, Attributes, and Feelings

It's springtime; you feel more energetic, optimistic, and creative, almost unstoppable. You are surrounded by new life, blossoming trees, bright spring flowers, baby birds chirping, and insects humming. Your vegetable garden is yielding beyond expectation; flowers and shrubs are vibrant and colorful. You are surprised, given how impossible it looked last winter – overgrown with weeds, soggy from the incessant rain, and covered in rubble.

I like to use the analogy of gardening – and not just because I love springtime. It's because the creation of your empowered, joyful life is similarly about expectations of new beginnings. To recap what I mentioned in the Introduction, I've often heard that many self-help books and workshops do not meet expectations or deliver on their promises. The main reason is that they suggest it's possible to make sustainable change using infertile soil. Preparing the soil is fundamental. That inevitably involves both *weeding* and *seeding*.

Similarly, when you hold the conscious intention to initiate change, those impediments – namely corrosive emotions, limiting beliefs, and painful memories – need to be pulled from their roots and replaced with the creative concepts and emotions you aspire to; those which will reflect your best life, your freedom. It all starts with your story.

ADDING DEFINITION AND CONTEXT TO YOUR STORY

You probably already know what has been holding you back and why you are reading this book in need of change – although sometimes it feels confusing, and you can't quite get your head around it. Where to start? The most effective way to commence healing is to write – whether on an electronic device or by putting pen to paper – even though you would rather avoid bringing painful memories to mind. Committing something to the written word sends a message to your subconscious that you are no longer procrastinating; you're ready to move forward. It also helps bring clarity, perspective, and a sense of control. As you add context and definition, you will discover that fear and anxiety subside; the challenge becomes manageable. Following is a case study from my files.

CASE NOTES **MEET ABELLA**

Abella, now in her early forties, is one of three siblings; the others are both brothers. She proved to be the brightest and most resourceful child from an early age and developed a strong attachment to both parents equally. Each was successful in their respective careers: one as an accountant, the other as a physiotherapist. Their expectations of all three children were high, particularly with regards to scholastic achievement. Being a natural-born athlete, Abella was encouraged to study hard and train rigorously, and that inevitably led to her life being micromanaged by her parents. She graduated university summa cum laude and achieved state, then national status in her sport. Predictably, by her late twenties, she was mentally and physically exhausted. Having been denied the freedom of both social and more intimate interactions outside the family unit throughout her childhood and teens, she was unsuspecting and vulnerable. She described her first marriage to a totally unsuitable partner as "an act of obedience". She persevered for six years before finding the courage to file for divorce and has since remarried. Having no success with traditional medications, she came to see me for a "different perspective".

Physical Symptoms: Included excessive hair loss, chronic indigestion and nausea, high anxiety, low energy levels, short temper, disrupted sleep patterns, and back pain, although extensive medical testing had found no evidence of disease.

Abella's Beliefs and Behaviors:

- I need to be "taken care of"; I can't function successfully on my own.
- There's a price to pay to be taken care of – and that is complete obedience and accommodating my carer's needs.
- My opinions have no value.
- It's disloyal for me to think I am entitled to a voice.
- It is my husband's responsibility to make me happy.
- Love actually means submission.

- Being loved is conditional upon achievement/success.
- I am helpless to make changes in my life.
- I am incapable of effective, independent decision making.

She also admitted to being highly critical of anyone with different standards and values, and to having unrealistic expectations of family members and friends – which caused her to feel constant frustration and disappointment with them.

Abella's Corrosive Emotions and Attributes:

Overwhelmed	Disappointed	Repressed
Confused	Trapped	Betrayed
Resentment	Unappreciated	Frustrated
Unacknowledged	Judgmental	Helpless
Unhappy	Anxiety	Anger

SUCCESSFUL OUTCOMES (WITHIN TEN WEEKS)

- Relief of all emotional symptoms, and over 80% decrease in the intensity/presence of all physical symptoms
- Able to more easily acknowledge and express emotions to family
- Unconditional acceptance of self and others

- An understanding that she is loved by her husband and children for who she is, not for what she has achieved academically or otherwise
- Gratitude and appreciation replaced the tendency to be critical and judgmental
- Significant improvement in (all aspects) of the marital relationship
- Reprioritization of marriage over further professional development (major shift in focus)
- Increased ability to engage in and initiate spontaneous activities with family
- Encouraging and consistent support from all family members
- Increased self-esteem and a real sense of belonging within a cohesive family unit

Now it's your turn.

EXERCISE: HOW DID I GET HERE?

- List a few life-altering events, traumas, or major decisions you've made that have had unexpected or unwanted consequences, which you believe are keeping you from living your best life.
- Reduce the narrative for each one to bullet-point format to help clarify your thoughts and be specific. No need to analyze them all just yet.
- Take just *one* of those setbacks and break it down into a format as I've done in Abella's case study, with the emphasis on corrosive emotions, beliefs, attitudes, and behaviors.

- As you add context and definition, you will discover that fear and anxiety subside; the challenge becomes manageable.

We initiate change by processing emotions and knowing that emotions, feelings, and trauma anchor and shape our core beliefs, attitudes, and behaviors. Being able to identify those emotions properly and understand their source diminishes their power and hold. The next page contains an inventory of over one hundred words categorized as Corrosive Emotions and Attributes to help you define and communicate your experiences. They are representative of commonly shared experiences, but by all means, use your own alternatives. By and large, we use the same words over and over because that's what we're used to, though they often don't express the breadth of how we are feeling. For example, you will find several words that define feelings of anger. That is because the interpretation of words is subjective. It is influenced by your family's language, your education, your cultural heritage, media speak, tag lines, pop-culture, and social media. One or more words for anger will resonate with you more strongly than others. For other people, that same word will not resonate at all although they had the exact same experience.

BEST USE OF EMOTION AND BELIEF INVENTORIES

- Read each segment of the inventory *mindfully* more than once. Hover over the words to encourage a connection to your subconscious. When your body and mind are relaxed, you will be surprised to find more words than expected leap off the

EMOTIONS, ATTRIBUTES, AND FEELINGS

page for your attention. Add them all to your list. This step is an important part of the *weeding* process.
- Switching off the noise in your head allows a clearer connection to your subconscious. That can happen within a very short space of time, in minutes.
- But, as you are just beginning to learn a new way of being, it is best to set aside dedicated, uninterrupted time to heal your body, mind, and spirit. Sixty to ninety minutes gives you time to identify underlying feelings and misguided beliefs, engage in the exercises, and remain focused. It also eases the body into a relaxed state, allowing you to gather creative momentum. The sooner you replace those rigid neural pathways with invigorating, unpolluted Life-Affirming Choices, the sooner you will be living your best life.

NOTE: For the best effect, I recommend you do not commence any of the following exercises until you have read this entire chapter.

IDENTIFYING CORROSIVE EMOTIONS, FEELINGS & ATTRIBUTES

CONFLICT	RESENTMENT	INDIFFERENCE
defeated	hurt	pessimistic
helpless	cynicism	apathy
frustrated	grudge	callousness
burdened	unappreciated	unfeeling
crushed	maliciousness	complacence
antagonistic	contempt	immobilized
victimized	irritation	disinterest
competitive	wounded	insensitive
attacked	spitefulness	disconnected
disharmony	offended	disregard
disagreement	slow burn	

SEPARATION	ANGER	AGGRESSION
ignored	incensed	sarcasm
sadness	animosity	withholding
rejection	bitterness	belligerent
unloved	exasperated	intentional harm
unlovable	outraged	violation
unheard	antagonistic	vindictive
deserted	disgust	resistance
loneliness	aggravated	repulsed
alienated	indignant	assault
uncared for	loathing	venom
unacceptable	acrimony	hatred
unimportant		

EMOTIONS, ATTRIBUTES, AND FEELINGS

INFERIORITY	GRIEF & GUILT	DISEMPOWERED
impotent	distressed	manipulated
unworthy	remorse	threatened
hopeless	heartache	frightened
pathetic	shame	directionless
unacceptable	blame	dominated
unwelcome	disgrace	loss of identity
incompetent	regret	subdued
second-rate	self-pity	overlooked
defective	dishonored	trapped
inadequate	liability	repressed
flawed	stigma	abused
stupid	penitent	confused
overwhelm		

WHAT'S CAUSING THE MOST STRESS?

A rating scale makes it easier to prioritize which emotions, feelings, and attributes are causing the most stress. Use a scale where the strongest resonance is 10, and the least is 1. Our goal here is first to weed out those feelings that no longer support your goals, and then if you feel it necessary, to seed their opposite.

Access to how you are *really* feeling, even if you've been suppressing those feelings for years, is sometimes easier if you listen to the voice in your head, your self-talk. Here's a condensed example of a scenario I have heard more times than I can remember. Let's say you really want a long-term relationship, but up until now, you haven't been able to get past the first six months, or even less. You are angry, hurt, disappointed, bruised, and ready to give up dating for the umpteenth time. You thought you learned something from the last one, but no, you are back on that same old treadmill.

Your **self-talk/beliefs** sound something like this:
What's wrong with me?   It's my fault things never work out.
I am nothing without a partner.   I'm not enough.
I'm unattractive, too ordinary.
I'm too needy, or I'm too sensitive.
Relationships are not worth the effort.
I am unlovable.

The associated **emotions** constantly wearing you down, feel like this:
Stupid / self-punishing / embarrassed – Rating Scale 8/10
Second-rate / unimportant / pathetic – Rating Scale 8/10
Incapable / defective / unwanted – Rating Scale 6/10
Helpless / frustrated / misunderstood – Rating Scale 10/10
Defenseless / disempowered / confused – Rating Scale 9/10
Unacknowledged / unworthy / boring – Rating Scale 7/10

EXERCISE: RATING EMOTIONAL INTENSITY

As you can see, some emotions/feelings have a stronger hold on you than others, depending on how long you have been repeating the negative self-talk, how long you have been re-living the same type of relationship, and how deeply committed you were to each partner. I have found it most effective to process one emotion at a time. Why? Because each has a unique point of origin (energetic

EMOTIONS, ATTRIBUTES, AND FEELINGS

imprint), and *your subconscious responds best to simple, specific, short instructions*. Let's do it!

- Disconnect from your external world. Prepare your environment to best support your creative endeavor. Ideally, that means you switch off devices (or set to silent mode) and remove them from arm's length, so you won't be tempted to check them. You cannot be in your subconscious and conscious simultaneously. It's like trying to have a light on and off at the same time. It can't happen.
- Connect to your inner world. If you can do that easily, that's great. If not, find a quiet space where you won't be interrupted to complete both Easy Mindful Meditation and Conscious Connection. The good news is that once the integration processes have taken firm hold in your neural pathways, or if you have already learned to retreat deep into your inner world at will, you can skip right by this hoop. You will be joining the ranks of countless others who can silently integrate their transitions in seconds, while riding on a bus, walking down the street, sitting at the library, or just enjoying a quiet cup of tea.
- To help you get a more accurate reading of your discomfort level, close your eyes, repeat the emotion slowly and quietly to yourself two or three times with your dominant hand on your solar plexus. Allow the numeric rating to arise from your subconscious *without trying to force it*. Don't allow your conscious mind to slip into analytical mode, because that is what it will want to do instinctively. Instead, relax, breathe, be patient, remain connected.

- If you can't decide the rating, it's helpful to repeat two words for comparison. Write a rating next to each corrosive emotion on your list before you go to the next step. Be patient with yourself; remember that your mind and spirit are not accustomed to digging deeper; they are stuck and resistant. They're used to quick and easy – and that's not working!

EXERCISE: HOW TO ACTIVATE WEEDING SCRIPTS

We refer to Corrosive Emotions as impediments that represent anything that stands in the way of your goals and limits your capacity to create a new path. All scripts in this program pay homage to Universal Intelligence (or however you define the Ultimate Power of Creation). They reinforce your intentions. They acknowledge that the impediment has served a purpose, its purpose is now understood, the lesson learned, and you are no longer bound to it.

To start, let's look at where you want to be, based on your goals for the future, as we include reference to them in this next exercise. Imagine your entire life as a wheel, divided into equal segments. Each segment represents an aspect of your life. In real time, different aspects of your life will take precedence over others at different times. For most of us that is normal, predictable, and manageable, provided any glaring imbalance is short-lived. A balanced life is, more often than not, a healthy, happy one. Often, the simple act of recreating the wheel on paper, will identify areas that need your attention. The segments I have listed below have served the purpose so far, though you may prefer to rename them. Perhaps try a few of the exercises using the pre-set categories before making any change.

EMOTIONS, ATTRIBUTES, AND FEELINGS

- Life Goals (all encompassing)
- Relationship and Family
- Work and Professional Development
- Optimal Health and Fitness (includes Personal Growth)
- Recreation and Social Engagement
- Faith and Spirituality

Using the example on the next page, in the Script for Release of Corrosive Emotions, you will see it refers to *rejection* as an *impediment to my goals of Family and Relationship*. If, on the other hand, the impediment is impacting your entire life, you would choose Life Goals as your frame of reference. However, I have found the more specific your reference, the more effective the release.

Just for a moment, let's revisit a few critical aspects of the creative process detailed in Chapter 4, where you learned that profound, lasting change to our thought patterns and emotions *can only be made through a connection to the subconscious*. Also, that you need to play the role of Observer to initiate change at that level. We have now arrived at that part of the creative process that requires you to do just that. It is fundamental to your success. Each time you repeat a script, you will close your eyes to observe your transition in action. The visual that arises may present as an object or environment that changes content, form, or color. We also know that *your subconscious will respond instantly* because it can't tell the difference between a real-time or a virtual experience.

There are a few ways you can approach the exercises and transitions in this book. Choose the one that resonates most strongly.

- **Option 1:** Recall a scenario or event that has special meaning. Remember Stephanie who loves to cycle on the weekend? Stephanie starts her transition by visualizing herself (as the Observer) at home feeling gloomy and lazy. Next, she is shopping downtown for bright, new cycling shorts and a jersey, until she finds the perfect look. When she does, she feels instantly energized and radiant – the blue mood has lifted. She heads for home feeling refreshed, optimistic, and happy. The corrosive emotions keeping her stuck no longer resonate, and fresh, creative concepts emerge in their place. A surge in her levels of dopamine and serotonin saved the day. She reassesses her 0-10 rating and is surprised at how low it has dropped on the scale, or that she can no longer connect to it.

- **Option 2:** If you are a creative spirit and practice yoga or meditation, your experience might be quite different, as you are accustomed to just *being* without effort or trying to construct an outcome. Your transition could be like many of my clients who are presented with swirls of vibrant rainbow colors or bright pulsating light, or others who feel waves of healing energy running from head to toe. Be patient; just observe it, and you'll know when the process is complete. Each of us is unique, so allow your imagination to take you where you need to go and trust it.

Finally, here it is. And, by the way, please remember I said that, provided you allow yourself to relax, detach from busy-ness, and follow the scripts as given, these protocols work.

EMOTIONS, ATTRIBUTES, AND FEELINGS

RELEASE OF CORROSIVE EMOTIONS

I acknowledge my feelings of <u>being disempowered as an impediment to my goals of Family and Relationship</u>, so now release them from their earliest point of origin, from every aspect of my life, and across all dimensions of time. I am supported by the Universe in this choice.

When the release is complete, you will feel different, usually lighter, freer. Often, there will be a huge shift in your emotions, energy levels, or state of mind. You might feel suddenly tired or relaxed. If you feel weepy, allow the tears to come without suppressing them. Our goal is always to relieve the body of its burden, in whatever way it deems appropriate.

REASSESS RATING ON 0-10 SCALE

Take a minute, settle into your body, and breathe gently. Don't be surprised if you discover the rating has dropped to 1 or 2 immediately, or the emotion no longer resonates. Alternatively, you could feel a slight twinge or more definite awareness of residual emotion. For example, the resonance has slipped from 8/10 to around 3/10, and something is still niggling.

The reason could be one or more of the following.
- There may be other emotional impediments linked to the one you are attempting to release. For example, on reflection you realize *being invisible*, which you initially rated 10/10, and on completion of the script, you reassessed as 4/10, is linked to

your experiences of being *rejected.* When you release *rejection,* the rating 4/10 for *being invisible* has totally cleared.
- You might need more practice, have missed a step, or have rushed it.
- You are being sabotaged by fear-based resistance.

OVERCOMING FEAR-BASED RESISTANCE

Resistance is fear-based, though consciously we don't always recognize it. You might think the reason you are procrastinating has to do with the fact that you feel constantly overwhelmed, confused, or you are "just not ready" for change. Or you may convince yourself you need to wait on something else to happen before you can commit to change. Avoidance comes in many disguises. On a subconscious level, you are either afraid of what the future might look like when you make a change, or you are holding on to a fear of losing the perceived benefits associated with your current state of being.

CASE NOTES   MEET MARYANNE

My client Maryanne is one of many examples. Maryanne had been suffering emotionally and physically for over a decade. Since her health declined, she has become the center of attention within a family who had habitually spent much more time with Maryanne's two siblings and much less time with her. At work, because of her disability, she was given special consideration, and she took full advantage. She also used her condition to emotionally blackmail

EMOTIONS, ATTRIBUTES, AND FEELINGS

her on-again/off-again boyfriend. Anytime he told her he wanted to break it off, she suddenly had a serious health crisis. He stayed. She delighted in telling me that she made sure to use her wheelchair as a prop whenever she was out in public, whether needed or not. It never failed to generate the attention she was seeking.

What prompted her visits to my office was a directive from the health services department at her workplace. The accommodations they had been making were at risk of being discontinued if she could not demonstrate a genuine intention to improve her state of health. Over the time we worked together, she made steady progress. She had a brighter outlook on her future, became more agreeable and cooperative at work and at home, and physically more independent. Because she seemed so much happier and independent, visits by her parents and siblings began to taper off. Her employer and workmates stopped making excuses for her poor attitude, attention seeking, and lack of performance. As a result, Maryanne became angry. All she really wanted was to be in the spotlight, fussed over, and made to feel special. Her boyfriend finally cut ties. The last I heard from Maryanne was that she was looking for another job and no longer wanted to continue our sessions.

Ask yourself if there is any reason you are afraid of moving forward. It can help to recall earlier setbacks or life-changing events that created unwanted or unexpected challenges you may have been ill-equipped to handle at that time. Whether related to family and friends, broken relationships, struggles at work, relocation, the loss of someone dear to you, or other crisis, the basis of fear is the same.

The next chapter, Misguided Thinking and Core Beliefs, contains an extensive checklist of self-defeating beliefs specific to resistance and stagnation, which are associated with the following fears.

Fear of change. *What's the worst thing that could happen if my situation changes?*

- Fear of losing control
- Fear of criticism, disapproval
- Fear of rejection, alienation, separation
- Fear of failure or success
- Fear of other negative consequence

The script for releasing fear-based impediments below is short and to the point. Please apply the same principle as you process those from your own list. For best effect, link those to a specific category of life goals, as I've done in the example. Then return to your original list of setbacks to continue releasing other Corrosive Emotions and Attributes.

RELEASE OF FEAR-BASED RESISTANCE

I acknowledge my profound <u>fear of change as an impediment to my Life Goals</u>, so now release it, from its earliest point of origin, from every aspect of my life, and across all dimensions of time. I am supported by the Universe in this transition.

SUPERCHARGE YOUR LIFE WITH LIFE-AFFIRMING DOWNLOADS

More often than not, simply weeding the corrosive emotions, long-held traumas, and resistance-based fear is enough to initiate a return to your True Self. Your *new normal* state of being feels amazing, unbelievable. You are experiencing greater clarity of thought, and you feel energized, happier, in control, and relaxed.

However, there are situations where a person's ability to reconnect to ordinary life-affirming feelings has been severely impaired. They involve the deep-rooted impact of emotional, physical, or mental abuse, cases of rape and sexual abuse, long-term institutionalization, profound grief, abandonment, and other extreme circumstances. Children are most susceptible. These victims and long-term sufferers respond particularly well when the release of emotional impediments is followed by the powerful healing effects of Life-Affirming Choices. Let's revisit our gardening analogy. The soil has been cleared of all weeds, rocks, and debris, looks rich, and is now ready for seeding. You can already see some signs of greenery popping up. Because the garden was in such a sorry state for so long, you decide to add some super-charged fertilizer, so the new growth will be stronger, greener. Integrating Life-Affirming Choices regularly into your healing process has the same effect.

CASE NOTES   MEET DAVID

Though I have dealt with many such cases, one particular client comes to mind. David was a 27-year-old late-starter with the dream of becoming an IT consultant. He had immigrated years ago with his parents and three siblings from a small Eastern European town close to the Adriatic Sea to settle in Vancouver, BC. Working hard to put himself through university, he was proudly looking forward to graduation in a few months and the prospect of a full-time job. As the eldest of four children who had all been exposed to the gruesome consequences of political conflict and were still suffering the emotional and psychological effects, he was protective of his younger siblings.

Although similarly impacted, his parents resisted all attempts by immigrant service agencies to provide support, in the misguided belief that the children would eventually recover as they assimilated at school or within the broader community. That theory wasn't playing out too well. Understandably, David's parents were distrusting of authority, grieving, and still angry at being forced to leave their homeland. Their everyday conversation was dominated by old country political and social issues, the potential of new conflict, and worry about family members they had left behind, although there was no longer cause for concern. Unfortunately, they had brought the war with them, and those reminders continued to be a destabilizing influence on the children.

A depressed, frustrated David found himself at a crossroad, extremely conflicted between his devotion to his younger siblings who looked to him for support, loyalty to his parents who left everything behind to give their children a better life, and his yearning to live an independent life. He wanted to marry and have his own family. Caring and intelligent, he realized that in his current state of depression he was unlikely to achieve any of his goals. Interacting with others outside his own culture, expanding his English vocabulary, and adapting to new norms and values had proved overwhelming. He never smiled. University classmates considered him too serious, detached, and morose so didn't welcome him to social events, as they would have otherwise. Of course, they had no knowledge of his background. Perhaps if they had, they might have treated him differently.

EMOTIONS, ATTRIBUTES, AND FEELINGS

Guarded when we began, a few weeks into our sessions, David relaxed and was able to share details of his story. Growing up, neither he nor his siblings had known what it might be like to walk down the street without worrying they might be caught in crossfire, wounded, or killed, or that one or both parents would be lost to them. They had never felt safe, even within their family home. They trusted no one other than immediate family members. Predictably, living in limbo throughout many years of conflict took its toll, as the children became increasingly alienated from those life-affirming emotions we all take for granted.

Working with the inventory of Corrosive Emotions and Attributes helped David acknowledge the full range of emotional experiences he was suppressing. First, we cleared those and his fear-based resistance, using the preceding exercises and tools. By the end of the fourth session, he admitted to feeling much better: "No longer any heaviness in my chest...body feels lighter...I feel less overwhelmed...I'm sleeping better...my thoughts are clearer, and I am less pessimistic." It was reassuring to hear, but I knew it was not enough. He still wasn't smiling. What I wanted to hear were words like happy, hopeful, excited, and more. So, the next step was to have David review the inventory of Life-Affirming Choices. What were those attributes or concepts he couldn't relate to but would like to manifest in his best life?

Here's where you remember that *it is just as easy to introduce (seed) a new concept and emotion or reinstate a long-forgotten one to your neurons as it is to release anything undesirable.* This is precisely what we did – with great success. Soon after our sessions concluded, David decided it would be in his own best interests and that of his younger siblings to establish his own home base. "It will be a happier place for them to come whenever they need me and hopefully will improve my chances of finding a wife. I'm looking forward to the move."

HOW TO SEED LIFE-AFFIRMING DOWNLOADS

On the next few pages, you will find an inventory of Life-Affirming Choices, which contains over one hundred emotions and attributes to inspire you. No need to limit yourself to those though; I'm sure you can think of others. Their purpose is to accelerate growth and healing, and support your journey to an enlightened state of being as you live a more purposeful life.

To ensure the best-possible long-term result, please make sure you have *weeded* thoroughly before attempting this *seeding* exercise. Following the inventory are two optional scripts to help you integrate your Life-Affirming Choices. Here's a recap of the process:

- Take your time, relax. Select your preferences from the inventory, or from a personalized list.
- Choose the script that resonates most strongly, or do as I do, which is to alternate them depending on the context.
- It's the same process you used to release Corrosive Emotions, except that this time you will be in seeding mode, which means *receiving incoming data*, so your visualization or energy flow will likely change. That's fine.
- Close your eyes to become the Observer, and allow the process to unfold slowly and organically through to completion before opening your eyes.
- You will know instinctively when the download is complete.

EMOTIONS, ATTRIBUTES, AND FEELINGS

- I have found it most effective not to attempt too many at the same time, so I generally stick to one, maybe two, if the script is identical. The simpler, the better.

If your body's response to the script involves feeling, rather than visual content, you will likely start to feel almost instantly calm, more relaxed, and happier. Some people have been known to burst out laughing, others just to giggle, some cry happy tears. Others' response has been "What was I thinking?"

SUPERCHARGED LIFE-AFFIRMING CHOICES

CONFIDENCE	ACCEPTING	INTERESTED
faith	approval	kindness
conviction	consent	comforting
candor	amenable	agreeable
supportive	flexible	participatory
tenacity	affinity	welcoming
courage	compliance	attentive
nerve	approachable	empathy
certainty	corroboration	affection
affirmative	permission	friendliness
authenticity	open	curiosity
determination	adaptable	sympathetic
assertion	forgiving	responsive

EQUALITY	WILLINGNESS	CAPABILITY
similarity	readiness	competent
parity	free choice	inspirational
co-operative	consensual	effectiveness
impartial	hope	potential
agreement	delight	dynamic
tolerance	purposeful	skill
fair play	enthusiasm	enough
balance	inclination	suitable
equivalent	cheerful	creative
uniformity	intentional	intelligent
oneness	happiness	productive
congruity	persistent	power

EMOTIONS, ATTRIBUTES, AND FEELINGS

RESPECT	ENTHUSIASM	TOGETHERNESS
attentive	energetic	unified
caring	spontaneity	peaceful
concern	passion	connected
feeling	excitement	complementary
esteem	joyful	harmony
warmth	uplifting	closeness
appreciation	eagerness	supported
compassion	spirit	serene
deference	vivacity	affection
involvement	fun-loving	intimacy
dignity	exhilaration	loved
regard	inspiring	belonging

DOWNLOAD LIFE-AFFIRMING CHOICE (1)

I have a Universal perspective and understanding of what it feels like to be optimistic. It is safe and possible for me now to accept this attribute as my new reality.

OR

DOWNLOAD LIFE-AFFIRMING CHOICE (2)

Every cell in my body unconditionally accepts optimism as my new reality. It is now safe and possible for me to do so. I am supported by the Universe in this choice.

Supercharged seeding of Life-Affirming Choices can be done at any time after weeding Corrosive Emotions and Attributes. There's no need to wait until after you have extracted self-defeating beliefs or misconceptions, as presented in the following chapter. However, I highly recommend you process the beliefs related to fear-based resistance sooner than later. It will ease your way into the entire program.

A reminder: the key to achieving the best possible outcome in any aspect of this process is your willingness to surrender to its *absolute simplicity*. Set aside all preconceived ideas that solutions need to be complex, hard-learned, and rigid. None of that applies here. The more you over-think it, the less likely you will be to achieve your goals. On the next page you'll find a step-by-simple-step Process Overview which applies to all the core exercises you'll discover through to the last chapter.

EMOTIONS, ATTRIBUTES, AND FEELINGS

WEEDING AND SEEDING OVERVIEW

- Start with the exercises in Chapter 6, Accessing Your Creative Genius.
- Place yourself in a quiet, peaceful space free of any possible interruption. Relax, close your eyes, focus on your breath for a few minutes before you start the process.
- Write a bullet-point list of specific life-altering events and traumas, allowing space below each one.
- Add any negative emotions or feelings you can readily associate with those events, either as an immediate response or later consequence.
- Refer to the Inventories in any chapter to help you identify others that are likely lurking deep within.
- Connect to your feelings. Close your eyes, place the palm of your hand on your solar plexus. Choose one emotion from your list, and repeat it quietly until you connect with its physical resonance anywhere within your body. Rate its resonance on a scale of 1-10, with 10 being most resonant.
- Release (weed) or download (seed) each one using the appropriate script. Relax into the role of Observer, and take your time to allow the creative process to take full flow.
- Re-assess your progress on the 1-10 scale. A residual rating of 3 or more is an indication that another emotion is attached. Process it in the same way.

Chapter 8

Misguided Thinking and Core Beliefs

Believe it or not, it is just as easy to release self-defeating beliefs as it is to rid yourself of corrosive emotional baggage. It can also happen in the blink of an eye. This chapter talks about how we absorb environmental attitudes and behaviors, and how strongly we are influenced by our cultural collective. To help you get started on your vision of a brighter, more expansive future, I have included a checklist of common beliefs shared by so many others stuck in fear-based resistance and stagnation. It is perfect for those like me, who are prone to an overactive left brain. Truth be told, I should say I *was* stuck. Now, I'm fluid. Other, more specific checklists are included in the next section. You will find those in chapters titled Reclaim Your Identity and Self-Esteem, No More Secrets: Surviving the Aftermath of Abuse, De-Mystifying Eating Disorders and Weight Loss, and Embracing the Flow of Money and Abundance.

Like most people, you probably have no idea how or why something that happened twenty years ago and is now buried deep within your subconscious is shaping your present-day reality. Let's say your parents split when you were five years old, and you continued to live with your mom and siblings. That would have been a hugely painful and disruptive event. Within a few years, your mom remarried a partner who loved you and your siblings in a way you had never experienced with your dad. Your stepdad was protective, he listened, he was kind. Fast forward to today. Your recall of early events around your parents' separation is now quite vague, as are the feelings you experienced at the time, though the episode is still present in your subconscious.

The associations attached to your recall would be quite different had your mom not remarried happily to such a wonderful partner. Instead, let's say she had to struggle through many years of hardship on her own, with little emotional or financial support, or married someone who treated you all badly. Fast forward to a present-day reality based on that scenario, and you very likely have issues around intimacy, are closed off emotionally and scared of settling down, or are needy. Your relationships have so far been short-lived because you've developed a few really effective protective mechanisms to keep the possibility of emotional pain at bay. Or, you may have completely unrealistic expectations of what a relationship could and should offer. Yet, you are surprised no-one has "grabbed the brass ring".

PARALYSIS BY ANALYSIS

What I have learned over many years of hearing similar stories is that the *only* way to unravel the mysteries of the mind and return to a healthier way of living and interacting is to first identify the underlying emotional interference. However, for some readers, particularly those with left-brain orientation, I've needed to take a more indirect route. You may be one of these, whose way of processing information and events is practical and dominated by the neocortex part of the brain, which relates to cognitive thinking, decision making, planning, and belief systems. That's what you are most comfortable with and that's how you best express yourself. Of course, that is okay – unless you use it to mask or suppress your feelings, or as resistance to change, as I did for way too long. If so, access to your emotions, and perhaps even to this entire program, will be blocked by a heavy, locked soundproof door.

Not sure if you fit that profile? Do you recognize any of these avoidance techniques?

- The belief that you are incapable of change and healing (I've been stuck too long, tried other things, nothing works.)
- Lack of confidence in your ability to effectively put these protocols into action (lack of faith in your own ability to take charge of your life, to turn things around)
- Self-blame (It's my fault that I'm in this situation, maybe I deserve it.)
- Self-sabotaging behaviors (Anytime something good starts to happen, I mess it up.)
- Fear of an unknown future, or being too comfortable with your pain, or misguided self-protection (What will a different me look like? What will happen to my friendships and relationships? What will change bring with it?)

- The belief that there is no better version of yourself and no real possibility of a better quality of life (It's me against the world... I am unsupported by this so-called Universal energy or any such equivalent, so why keep trying?)

The good news is that the locked soundproof door can be flung wide open, just by a slight shift in perspective. To start the ball rolling, we will break down resistance with the same logic I have used successfully for countless others. You might be surprised at just how easy that is. Then we will explore the many ways your core beliefs have evolved, and why some have tighter control of you than others.

First, let's take you way back to your very beginning. Your birth. Do you still look like that, think like that, feel like that? Of course, you don't. Why? Because every part of you, every cell, every organ is dynamic and in a constant state of flux from day to day, from moment to moment. Admit it, you *have* changed. How painful was it? You are not even the same person you were when you first started reading this book. Your neural pathways have been adapting to a new perspective since that exact moment and will continue to do so. So, please don't allow a few random rigid thoughts to govern the entire trajectory of your life.

Next, that same newborn came prepackaged, untainted by life events, with innate intelligence, neurotransmitters, and hormones that drive it instinctively towards things that are good and steer it clear of anything that resembles a threat. We already know that has been proven by science. It's not until that newborn becomes exposed to external influences that this innocent enlightened being starts to morph into something else entirely. It begins to adapt to environmental conditions, sometimes adverse, from a very early age, which

MISGUIDED THINKING AND CORE BELIEFS

distorts its original outlook or inhibits its creative capacities. You are still in possession of that innate intelligence, regardless of how confused you may feel right now. That part of you that always strives for all that is good has placed this book in your hands. It was no accident, even if you choose to ignore it.

Next, *any* change in your life can produce what I refer to as *transitional discomfort* or emotional upset. Positive transformation is harmless; any associated discomfort is invariably momentary. It's called adjustment, adaptation, reshaping, expansion, wisdom, emotional growth. Do you still remember when, as a kid, every time you cried because you didn't get what you wanted? I didn't think so. My suggestion? Get over it, and get on with it.

Next. You know that air that you are breathing right now that's keeping you alive? That's the life force that I refer to as the Universe, Nature, Divine Intelligence, the Source of all Creation, and so on. That is the very same energy field that keeps rivers flowing, flowers blooming, birds flying, and the stars way up in the night sky where they belong. It has done so for centuries before you made your appearance and will continue long after you've departed. So, please tell me now that it doesn't exist. And, if it has supported you up until now, why would it stop?

Sure, you may have done or said some mean or vindictive things or been unkind, selfish, or just plain stubborn, as have we all. If you are feeling bad about yourself, it is not because you are being judged or punished by any form of higher power. It's because you have labeled yourself, or have been labeled by others, in ways you find offensive or just plain hurtful. That is what *really* makes you feel small and isolated.

Well, today is your lucky day. I've included a Self-Forgiveness script in this chapter, which I strongly recommend you complete, whether you think you need it or not, before moving on to reprogram the beliefs hampering your capacity for healing and transformation. Provided the guidelines have been followed, the Self-Forgiveness Script alone has proven to initiate a huge shift in mindset that can propel you forward.

Last, and far from least, are a few words from our most revered genius, Albert Einstein: "We cannot solve our problems with the same thinking we used when we created them."

THE ROLE OF CULTURE, TRADITIONS, AND TRENDS

Your beliefs and misconceptions all have a different point of origin, whether, like your emotions, they are stuck to you like a limpet to a rock or binding you with gossamer-fine threads. Most of us don't question their origin or validity until we are faced with a crisis; usually, it is one of identity. *Who am I? Where do I fit? Do I really belong here?* That process of introspection is healthy, provided it remains life-affirming, open, and constructive. When we allow introspection to cross to the dark side – that is, filled with self-criticism, self-denial, suspicion, and paranoia – we are at risk of being preyed upon and manipulated by others less well-meaning. Even worse, is when such a mindset is linked to anxiety, depression, and suicide. The more discerning your thoughts and beliefs, the more enlightened your words and actions. So, it's worth looking at how those thoughts, beliefs, and misconceptions have brought you to this place, your present mindset.

MISGUIDED THINKING AND CORE BELIEFS

Even before you can speak as an infant, you begin to process information and events through your senses of smell, touch, hearing, and sight. Each experience forms an impression, wordlessly. Dependent upon their significance, you learn to communicate their importance by crying (for example, to express hunger, discomfort, or upset), which brings a response or reward. The foundation for future expression of those experiences is laid there, as are the belief systems that support them. Early-childhood events, when harmful to your well-being, give rise to self-protective coping mechanisms and maladaptive behaviors, which persist through to adulthood if left unattended. Those can also serve to suppress emotional pain incurred at their point of origin. Infants and children confronted with stressful situations mostly can't physically escape the source. The "fight or flight" response we engage in as adults is not an option. Typically, these children "freeze", become numb with shock, and withdraw emotionally within themselves. In cases of severe shock, some have become catatonic.

Later, we become aware of the influence of our cultural traditions and customs as a major influence on our lifestyle, psyche, and decision making. Your family might have Thanksgiving traditions that were started generations ago and are now set in stone as far as your family is concerned. Wherever family members are in the world, at Thanksgiving or Christmas, it is expected they all come together, and they almost always do. Perhaps it is the ritual of everyone getting together at Mom and Dad's for Sunday dinner or just a particular food that has special meaning.

On the upside, those traditions play a valuable role in creating cohesion and loyalty within the family structure. They reinforce family values, support the development of each member's identity and sense of belonging, and teach new generations about their culture and customs. Further, they provide an opportunity to share invaluable intergenerational bonding experiences. Your beliefs and aspirations about the value of family, what is right and good about sibling relationships, how to provide the best environment for your own children, and whether you even want children, start right there. Likewise, this is where your notions of how to treat others, how to respond appropriately to how they treat you, and your generalized worldview originate.

On the downside, here we are in the twenty-first century, where outdated and ill-serving traditions, values, and attitudes are still being used as social and political tools of repression and justification for inhumane and degrading acts of violence, particularly towards women. They are cited as a rationale for "honor killings" in India, Pakistan, and Afghanistan. In addition, according to recent statistics from the World Health Organization (WHO), these traditions place at risk the human rights of almost three million girls, ranging in age from infancy to fifteen years, who are born in Africa, the Middle-East, and Asia and subjected to the painful, life-threatening practice of genital mutilation. In countries where homosexuality is still viewed as a *moral* versus a *human rights* issue, the argument for traditional values has been used as an excuse to undermine, even negate human rights. In seventy countries, same-sex sexual activity is a crime; in six of them it is punishable by death.

Closer to home, fallout from the rigid mindset of white supremacy still dominates our newscasts and social media; hate crimes targeting African Americans and other minority groups remain an everyday occurrence. Those extremist ideologies are perpetuated because they serve the function of connecting believers to like-minded others, their adopted tribe. This attachment gives each member an elevated sense of purpose, inclusion, and importance, which subverts individual beliefs and values. Inevitably, in this environment, members' neural pathways are saturated with stress hormones that reinforce anxiety, fear, greed, materialism, and hatred. For some, there's no going back.

Less threatening, albeit equally binding, are our ties to political, social, sporting, or other associations that embrace their own traditions and codes of behavior to which all members are expected to adhere. Unwelcome consequences are meted to those who question their value or no longer want to conform. So, we adapt and modify our beliefs and behaviors in exchange for acceptance and inclusion.

Not all data you gather from the collective consciousness is as emotionally charged, though it can be disruptive to your mindset if you are not paying attention. As an example, when we continually hear comments from friends and associates or on social media that are intolerant of others' lifestyle choices and we don't speak out against them, we are at risk of accepting negative stereotyping as fact. At the same time, we generate a range of negative emotions that distort our vision and capacity for compassion. Fear, hostility, and suspicion cause us to become skeptical and mistrusting of any person we meet from those communities without just cause. We are disinclined to engage with them for all the wrong reasons.

DEPRESSION AND SOCIAL MEDIA

Another significant influence impacting our beliefs and expectations today, more than ever before, is the media. We have come to accept its many innovations as an integral part of our daily lives without giving too much thought to its reverberating effects, particularly that of social media which is now used by 82% of the US population. Globally, the largest of these platforms is Facebook, with more than 2.85 billion active users each month, followed by YouTube as the most popular video-sharing platform. According to the latest survey by Our World in Data (www.ourworldindata.org): "US adults spend more than 7 hours per day on digital media (apps and websites accessed through mobile phones, tablets, computers, and other connected devices such as game consoles)." It is broadly accepted by analysts that pandemic conditions contributed in major part to the uptick.

Social media is a brilliant idea. It has become an indispensable tool for those seeking and providing employment; businesses and professionals to raise their online profile; users wanting to share blogs, podcasts, pictures, music, and messaging with local as well as international connections; and to help families and friends stay connected. It is also a good source of information for just about anything, from an interesting new hobby, recipes for healthier food choices, the latest fashion trends, and our favorite movie and TV personalities – not to mention some infamous, incredulous political tweets.

On the flipside, there are shortcomings. Though not fully attributable to the medium itself, social media has spawned a huge audience who blindly accept what they see and hear as truth, without questioning its source or underlying intention. That has already proven dangerous, even fatal in some cases. Research into the phenomena of social media has discovered that this gross misinterpretation of reality is undermining teens and young adults' mental health on a global scale and has led to an unprecedented rise in eating disorders. World Health Organization reports that, on a global scale, approximately 70 million people have an eating disorder. In America alone, according to the Renfrew Centre Foundation for Eating Disorders, "Up to 24 million people struggle with anorexia, bulimia, or related eating disorders....and 90% of cases involve women between the ages of 12 to 25." Another study, published in the *American Journal of Psychiatry*, reveals that people with eating disorders have the highest mortality rate of all those suffering from mental illness. No doubt that fact will come as a surprise to many readers, though it shouldn't. You will find the associated checklist of self-defeating beliefs and misconceptions in the chapter titled De-Mystifying Eating Disorders and Weight Loss.

Other unwelcome consequences of such public exposure have destabilized our sense of personal safety, well-being, and self-identity, en masse. The need to constantly check in to news feeds and advertising content from our smartphone and other devices has become an obsession. Though not officially classified as a mental illness, FOMO ("fear of missing out") is shown to contribute to escalating anxiety and depression, and has become so prevalent that it can now be found in the Oxford dictionary. This addiction disrupts eating habits and sleeping patterns and reduces the likelihood of real-time human contact and meaningful interaction.

Steadily streaming into our awareness twenty-four-seven is the idealized version of North America's social scene. Instant happy snaps saturate our Instagram, Facebook, Snapchat, and Tumblr accounts, contributing to the illusion that everyone else's life is more exciting than our own. Inevitably that leads to the misconception that our life, or we as individuals, do not compare favorably. Perhaps, we're not wearing the latest designer gear; not being seen at the trendiest clubs, social events, or concerts; not driving an upscale motor; can't afford to take vacations overseas in some exotic location, and so on. The truth is that most people don't post negative, unhappy, or ordinary life events online – just those that show themselves in the best light.

FOMO does not discriminate. It effects mature adults and teens equally, reinforcing neural pathways fueled by stress hormones and creating feelings of anxiety, disconnection, despair, inferiority, and so on. Core beliefs and thought patterns are similarly sidetracked as we begin to see ourselves as second-rate parents, incapable of adequately providing for our children, and believe we are socially under-par, constantly being judged, and the list goes on. Family values and goals previously held in high regard are called in to question for no good reason, more so if we have young children or teens engaging in the same behavior.

Here's the reality, the dark side. Social and digital media in all its forms has been responsible for hijacking personal or more intimate details meant to be shared with a select few. Reputations have been irreparably damaged, and the most vulnerable have been subject to cyber-bullying, scams, and deception. Worse is the global uptick in online cases of child sexual exploitation, child pornography, and child luring since the onset of the COVID-19 pandemic. In addition to chat rooms, Facebook, Snapchat, and Instagram as common sources of child-at-risk activity, predators are known to infiltrate games such as Minecraft. All children are vulnerable. They no longer know what is real.

Any time we spontaneously modify our thinking, fall in line with what's trending, or succumb to pressure from other external influences, we place ourselves at risk of manipulation. "Everyone else is going along with it, so it should be okay." Often, if we were to take a moment to step back to get perspective and objectivity, we would realize that those beliefs and behaviors are not at all aligned to our personal best interests. Let's now get rid of whatever is not who you really are or want to be.

EXERCISE: MOVING FORWARD WITH SELF-FORGIVENESS

We begin to free you from distorted beliefs with the script for Self-Forgiveness. Yes, this step *is* so simple, provided of course you have taken the time to prepare your space and to relax. If needed, return to Easy Mindful Meditation in Chapter 6.

- Close your eyes, breathe normally, set your intention.
- After you have read the script, hold your focus within your body as the Observer. Take it slowly. Remember, change might manifest as a slight pain, a sense of anxiety in the area of the solar plexus, an awareness of colors changing, energy shifting in the body, a sound, or a visual exchange of some kind. Be patient, stay with it.
- If there is any sensation of pain or discomfort, then direct your breath to that area and continue to breathe normally until the sensation diminishes or disappears.
- Then check in. You should be feeling lighter and more optimistic and accepting of yourself.

SELF-FORGIVENESS SCRIPT

I have a Universal perspective and understanding of what it feels like to forgive myself totally and unconditionally for all past misguided thoughts, words, and actions. It is now safe and possible for me to do so.

OVERCOMING FEAR-BASED RESISTANCE AND STAGNATION

Sometimes, unbeknown to us, a war rages between our conscious awareness and a subconscious fed by past emotional history and social conditioning. This results in a sense of being "stuck". We can be over-the-moon happy about something that just happened or about the prospect of something equally wonderful in the future, while at the same time feeling apprehensive as the subconscious subtly starts to undermine our joy.

CASE NOTES   MEET LAUREN

Lauren made a radical decision in her thirties to quit her well-paid but not-so-inspiring job to become a full-time artist. She'd had a passion for painting and drawing since her teens. The hours she spent immersed in the creative process were precious. She came alive as she worked with luminous acrylics. She loved the smell of them and felt most at peace in her little studio. Her talent and commitment were self-evident and applauded by her art teachers and local artists who encouraged her to continue. Due to difficult circumstances at home at the time, Lauren felt it best to defer university until the family was in a more stable financial position. She never went, but kept painting.

When we met, she was a working artist, who had achieved national status with paintings exhibited in galleries across the US. Inquiries from overseas galleries had also recently been pouring in. Divorced after nine years of incompatibility, followed by a few years of singledom, she had connected about two years ago with a like-minded, creative soul who she was hoping to marry. Life was good: she enjoyed financial independence and all that it brought into her life; she was in perfect health and highly regarded in artistic circles.

What could go wrong? A few months before, almost overnight, her "creative juices had stopped flowing." She was distressed. In the past, dry spells had lasted no more than a week or two. Those times, she took leave of her studio to spend time out of town, and then came back a few weeks later refreshed and ready to work. This time was different. "It's been over two months since I've had any inclination to return to work, and I'm becoming more and more distressed. Life is slipping away. I can't see how I'll ever be the person I was or be able to maintain this lifestyle if I can't paint."

After a few sessions clearing away misguided beliefs and attitudes related to her mom and dad and Lauren's responsibilities as the eldest sibling, we discovered the underlying cause of her creative blockage. It seems that her current crisis emerged within a week of her recent marriage proposal, which she had joyfully accepted. That realization came as a great surprise because she was genuinely excited about the prospect of a long-term future with "such a loving, fun, and kind man." Obviously, not all of her was *as* excited. What had happened? Faced with this life-changing event, Lauren's "fight or flight" response had been subconsciously triggered by her past. She thought she had already dealt with the breakdown of her first marriage and had happily moved on. Not so. We found that her feelings towards her future life partner were totally at odds with her true thoughts about marriage, its obligations, and potential limitations.

LAUREN'S SELF-DEFEATING BELIEFS AND MISCONCEPTIONS:

Marriage equates to the deprivation of independence.
Marriage equates to less time for creative activity (particularly painting).
Marriage will be disruptive to my work-related travel plans.
Marriage is associated with extra responsibility and burden.
Marriage means I have to share my hard-earned wealth. (It's taken decades to build.)
Marriage puts my hard-earned financial status at risk (of being stolen).
Marriage places limitations on the enjoyment of other valued friendships.
Marriage puts me under scrutiny and makes me vulnerable to criticism and judgment.
Marriage equates to deception and betrayal.
Marriage equates to verbal and emotional abuse.
Marriage equates to always "waiting for the other shoe to drop".
When we live together, he'll discover I'm not the person he thought I was, so he'll leave. (Lauren believed her partner had her on a pedestal.)

MISGUIDED THINKING AND CORE BELIEFS

Within days of our last session, I had a call from a reinvigorated Lauren to share her excitement at commencing a vivid new canvas and her impending marriage.

Now it's up to you. Following is the Inventory of Self-Defeating Beliefs and Misconceptions, which we commonly create to justify underlying resistance and stagnation.

EXERCISE: SELF-DEFEATING BELIEFS AND MISCONCEPTIONS

- Make a list of those that resonate with you, and then start the weeding process with just one. The script to release them follows.
- Getting started. Please stick to the original core script and keep the optional content short and on point. It works and is easy.
- Take your time to weed out any of the listed beliefs and others that might come to mind during your process. Simply replace the underlined content with a few words of your own.
- This script will weed out any belief, misconception, or attitude you feel is holding you back. Most beliefs, attitudes, and misconceptions clear instantly.
- How will you know if it worked? Because when you repeat that same statement to yourself, it no longer makes sense or, as it happens with many of my clients – there is spontaneous laughter!
- For best effect, be consistent with your practice, not scattered. Remember, when you first start, you are attempting to retrain your brain to alleviate the effects of accumulated stress hormones flooding your stubborn, old neural pathways

and to create new pathways. That's why setting aside a block of time dedicated to *weeding* and *seeding* is the most useful thing you can do. The results will become immediately apparent. Thorough weeding clears your space energetically and emotionally to seed Life-Affirming Choices and Creative Downloads in place of the weeds.

MISGUIDED THINKING AND CORE BELIEFS

RESISTANCE & STAGNATION
SELF-DEFEATING BELIEFS

- Change is difficult/too hard for me.
- I'm not sure the time is right; I'll wait till I feel better.
- I've created this mess I'm in; I have to live with it.
- Nothing has helped me before; I'm sure this program can't either.
- It sounds too simple to actually work.
- I'm too stuck in my ways to be able to change.
- It's impossible to let go of my past.
- My mind won't let me relax.
- I don't learn new stuff easily, even if it is simple.
- I'll have to work really hard to make it work.
- It will take up too much of my time.
- My friends and family will judge me and will think I'm crazy.
- Even if it does work, the benefits probably won't last long.
- I'm not convinced this is program is safe.
- I'm not a decisive person.
- Most people live life as unhappily as I do.
- It's not safe for me to connect with my emotions.
- I'm trapped.
- I feel like giving up.
- If I make these changes, I will regret it later.
- I'm not a creative person, so I won't be able to complete these exercises.
- It's easier for me to stay stuck
- My situation will never change.

- I don't deserve to heal and change; I've done some stupid things.
- Every time I try to do something good, it goes sideways.
- It might work for other people, but not for me.
- Boundaries alienate people.
- I wish I had someone else's life.
- If I just stay where I am, I'll be safer.
- I am unsupported by the Universe/God

RELEASE OF SELF-DEFEATING BELIEFS

The concept that <u>it sounds too simple to actually work</u> no longer serves my best interests. I release it now from every cell of my body, every aspect of my life, and across all dimensions of time. I am supported by the Universe in this transition.

Congratulations! You have conscientiously powered through the release of your worst fears and other corrosive emotions, unhappy memories, and misguided beliefs. You are now feeling more connected to your authentic self, happily creative, and awesome! You'll love this next exercise.

BONUS EXERCISE: SUPERCHARGED CREATIVE DOWNLOAD SCRIPTS

- Here's an opportunity to sprinkle stardust on your newfound Self! Note that the following script for Creative Downloads will be most effective when you've processed the worst of your corrosive emotions and misguided beliefs.

- Remember the Downloads for Life-Affirming Choices of positive, creative feelings in the previous chapter? The same concept and process applies to beliefs. Instead of weeding (releasing) redundant attributes, you will be seeding (introducing/reprogramming) new concepts and beliefs.
- Let's take an example from the beliefs associated with Resistance and Stagnation – "I'm too stuck in my ways to be able to change." Using that example, you could replace it with: "I am open to receiving new information. I'm adaptable." Another belief from that same list – "It's impossible to let go of my past" – could become, "It's possible and safe for me to let go of my past now," or "It's safe for me to move forward. I'm ready." Here's the script I use.

CREATIVE DOWNLOADS FOR BELIEFS AND ATTITUDES

I have a Universal perspective and understanding of what it is to know without any reservation that it is possible and safe for me to let go of my past now.

For practice, you might like to try a few of these before deciding on a personalized list.

- Instant change/transition/healing is possible for me/safe for me.
- It's possible for me to connect equally effectively to my right as to my left brain. It is safe for me to do so now.
- I give myself permission to embrace change now. It is safe to do so.

- Positive new thought and experiences are interesting and fun.
- Appropriate boundaries are beneficial to my well-being.
- I accept responsibility for my mistakes, have forgiven myself, and am ready to move on.

There's no limit to what you can do with these downloads. Focus on your goals and aspirations. What do you want to be, and what do you want to see in your best life?

The next section of the book specifically addresses emotional trauma and misguided thought patterns arising as a consequence of abuse, loss of self-esteem, eating disorders and weight loss, and financial insecurity. Advanced Integration Scripts follow these chapters.

freedom from deception and disinformation

"Whatever you can do, or dream you can, begin it. Boldness has genius, power, and magic in it."

Johann Wolfgang von Goethe

Chapter 9

Reclaim Your Identity and Self-Esteem

The combined elements of an internalized positive self-identity, or self-concept, and externalized acceptance within broader social settings form the attribute of self-esteem. Low levels of self-esteem, caused by the absence or distortion of either element in adolescence, are shown to be predictive of a reduced quality of life in adulthood. Consequences range from disruption to normal brain function, impaired language and cognitive development, delayed socio-emotional adjustment, depression and anxiety, avoidance of attachment, addictive behavior, poor cardio-respiratory health, criminal activity, and chronic unemployment in adulthood.

In an *ideal* world, by the time you reach high school, you have had enough practical experience with interpersonal relationships to prepare you for their challenges, disappointments, and surprises. When effectively connected within a well-functioning family, you understand the need for structure in your daily routines, respect preordained domestic and institutional rules, can adapt to changing situations, and are sensitive to the needs of others. Securely attached to your caregivers and clan, you feel valued and respected, and you understand how to express meaning and emotion appropriately. Yours is a safe, loving home to retreat to at the end of each day. The seeds of a positive self-identity have been sown.

Externally, as you interact with fellow students, friends, and work colleagues, you develop a positive social profile and healthy self-esteem. You are confident without being cocky, decisive without being dogmatic, considerate without being over-accommodating, open to constructive criticism without being hypersensitive, and can learn and move on from mistakes and failures. You are not susceptible to the manipulation of others. Despite everyday challenges, you remain optimistic on your way to meeting your life goals.

SHAPES AND SHADOWS

If I had found myself in front of a child psychologist earlier than I did, which was in my mid-teens, maybe things would have taken a different turn. Knowing why, at around five years of age, I'd ripped the clothes and long blond wig off my doll and scratched the cuteness off her face would likely have shaped my identity in another way. What remained of my night-time companion from which I had been inseparable was a soft, cuddly, cloth-filled shape of a body attached to a faceless plaster head. The original had been a mirror image of my mother: an attractive, outgoing, long-haired blond, with a great singing voice and always fashionable in her tailor-made wardrobe. She was popular and seemingly "loved by all", except possibly by Dad and most definitely not by me.

RECLAIM YOUR IDENTITY AND SELF-ESTEEM

For reasons not fully known to this day, my mother's aversion to accepting my existence as a meaningful element of her own was clear. Perhaps mine was an unwanted pregnancy. Who knows? Perhaps I was a reminder of a particularly unhappy period within their tension-filled, mismatched marriage. Their tension and anxiety fueled my own. The arguments we were exposed to before their year-long separation were loud enough to frighten and confuse. During the fights, I'd go hide in my closet because it shocked me to hear Dad raise his voice. Unlike his siblings who quickly made their presence felt, he was by nature reserved and quietly spoken.

Aside from the absence of parental harmony, the sense that something was amiss in my young world was evident to anyone who cared to take notice. No one did. I felt betrayed and confused by the fact that my sisters' relationship with my mother differed vastly from my own. Barely tolerated, I was more often criticized or ignored and kept at arm's length physically and emotionally by my mother, while my sisters enjoyed a warmer, respectful, and affectionate connection. They seemed much happier. I didn't blame them even though I was constantly compared to my first-born sister and found to be wanting. The only way I can explain my experience is to say I was living on the edge of a reality that wasn't mine, peering in. I was something akin to the understudy of the lead actor in a film or play, hoping for the chance to make my presence felt. At times I entertained the thoughts that: *I must have been misplaced at birth… I really belong to a more loving family… My real mother will come soon to whisk me away, and I'll be welcomed with open arms.*

By the time I was ten, I was considered to be a "moody, uncooperative" child, as though my profound sadness at being rejected was completely unrelated to my non-existent relationship with my mother. I existed in a bubble of uncertainty and disappointment, but I went about our shared family routines as was necessary to keep the peace. Anyone looking in from outside would see me as an integral part of the picture-perfect family. I'm there, front and center, in some happy snaps taken outside our church with Nonna, my maternal grandmother; a few with my cousins at the beach carrying brightly colored sand buckets and looking cute in one-piece togs; and others of us all prancing around Nonna's huge front garden. I understood even then that my mother's public displays of affection were contrived and fleeting, a face-saving gesture for the camera. The times in between those photos, the longest times, when I was made to feel I didn't belong, I had been banished to a black hole.

As my sense of isolation grew, I became increasingly resentful, resistant, and attention-seeking in a misguided effort to have my emotional needs met. Direct access to my father was limited, mostly out of consideration for his long working hours. Mother was the conduit of all matters domestic except for the occasional angry or frustrated outbursts at the dinner table by me. If Dad was aware of mother's indifference towards me in those early days, I couldn't say, though he was forced to come to terms with it a few years later.

Of course, there were some genuinely happy times. For me, other than climbing trees and riding my bike around the neighborhood with the three Taylor brothers who lived next door, those times were at school. I took refuge in books and learning, which proved to be my saving grace and a passion that continues to this day. There is still something unique about a well-written book that goes way beyond its words, intention, and the feel of it. It casts a spell. Doing well at school was important. There, I was accepted by those in authority. Both the Catholic school and college I attended were run by caring supportive nuns and lay teachers who instilled the belief that my contributions, ideas, and efforts were meaningful and that I had inherent value. That belief made me more determined to excel both academically and on the basketball court. Each success brought a sense of accomplishment and pride, albeit fleeting, though did little to repair the damage done at home, where I was frequently criticized. Neither parent ever attended my school or sporting events; "too busy." I envied those cousins whose parents would always go to cheer them on and show off their awards when we went to visit.

In contrast, when I proudly announced that I had won a scholarship for a year's advanced tuition, in her typical fashion, my mother was firstly dismissive, then skeptical, and then straight out called me a liar. As close as I got to congratulations was: "I'll call the school tomorrow to check that you are telling the truth." I should have expected nothing different. Though, as stupid as it sounds, despite all evidence to the contrary since infancy, I still harbored the hope that this achievement might be the turning point, that she would be proud, and would accept me as she did my siblings. What on earth was I thinking? I've since been blessed to learn that the source unconditional love and acceptance is not limited to familial relationships; it surfaces when and where you least expect it. Also, even more important is that hope really does spring eternal to help keep us afloat.

The abiding friendships often forged at school were beyond my capability. First, because the dire need to prove myself as worthy and capable drove me to be competitive, which worked, except that it made me not so popular either in the classroom or on the basketball court. Second, I had little genuine, relevant experience of the types of positive emotions and interactions that constitute healthy bonding. More familiar was the expression of angry, unforgiving emotion. Where there should have been some sense of how to engage appropriately with others, there was a vacuum. And thanks to my mother, I was acutely aware of being flawed and already socially awkward and cautious of new people. When, on the rare occasion, a classmate showed interest in developing a friendship, in my neediness, I overstepped the mark. My response was to become too quickly attached, possessive, and jealous that this person might be taken from me or reject me outright when they came to know me better. And, of course, they did. It was confusing and distressing. So, I kept to myself and became more withdrawn. The opportunities to form those life-long connections, which my sisters did, some of which they have to this day, had passed.

Of the people in my world who showed me any regard in those years, Dad and Nonna were favorites. I felt intuitively that Dad cared even though he wasn't openly affectionate. As a kid, there were special moments only we shared. Every so often, when he had time away from work, he let me hang out with him in his workshop or ride with him when he was on an errand. Nonna was a favorite because she was a constant – a safe, welcoming place to be. She did what all good grandmothers do – provide unconditional love and acceptance – and of course, my very favorite food, warm egg custard made from scratch topped with slices of banana. She remained the one constant and loving attachment I had until the day she died.

At age fourteen, this is what I knew to be true about my self-identity:

It is fragile at best, non-existent at worst. I am moody, frustrated, lonely, flawed, unacceptable, and I hate my mother. I am so angry and sad about this that I want to scream. I have no idea how to turn things around, or if it is possible to turn them around. And do I want to? I am unloved and clearly unlovable. I am often reminded I am a misfit. I wish I had a friend to talk to. When I am obedient, life is better than when I'm not, but I am more inclined to be defiant and stubborn. I daydream about running away; I don't know where to, or who to, just that I don't want to be here. I won't give in to my mother's demands for respect and compliance. She gives me nothing; I owe her nothing. Chronic indigestion and constipation, in every sense of that word, is part of my everyday reality. I also know that I need to take care of myself because no one else will. No one can be trusted. There's no point in complaining or sharing news, good or bad; no one will care or help. People don't understand me, nor are they interested in getting to know what's really going on, so it's best I keep my distance.

On the upside, I am smart, love to read and learn, get good grades, and don't like to fail. I am cute – not adorable, just pretty. I like climbing trees, have boundless energy, am curious, am good at basketball and tennis, don't like playing the piano, though I love listening to music. It's soothing. I wasn't good at math until I had a private tutor, a semi-retired Jewish accountant, who came after school and was always served sweet white coffee and biscuits.

The most damaging outcome of my mother's neglect is the sense of detachment that persisted well into adulthood. As a teen, though I appeared cold and disinterested, that wasn't me at all. I craved affection and physical reassurance that I was loved. Without any awareness of how to negotiate strangers in the outside world and blinded by the craving to fill that emotional void, I was susceptible to the sway of anyone with harmful intentions.

STRANGER THINGS

When I was around thirteen, I required treatment for ingrown toenails and was taken to visit a local chiropodist. He was around fifty years old then, with a thin face and thinning hair – a well-respected member of the community. When I arrived for my second appointment, he put his arm around my shoulders and told me, "You are much prettier than the other little girls who come here," and that I was "special" to him. It was odd, but I didn't think too much of it. On the next or subsequent visit, he hugged me when I entered his office, repeated that I was his "special girl" and then went about doing what he was being paid to do. Leading up to that visit, I had been having a particularly distressing time with my mother. Feeling fragile, between sobs, I shared a little of what had been going on at home. He was sympathetic and assured me whatever I shared would remain only between us. Also, I should know that he was there any time for me to talk to because I was his "special girl", though we should keep it a secret. He sat me on his lap and started stroking my hair, telling me I was too pretty to be hurting, reassuring me that he – "call me 'Uncle Dave'" (not his real name) – was there for me. It felt a little strange, but not threatening. Remember, I didn't know what appropriate affection was at that point. I was just grateful that someone cared enough to listen.

His routine greeting gradually escalated to a close hug and kiss on the cheek when I arrived, each time reminding me that everything that happened in his room was not to be shared with anyone. While he was tending my feet, we would talk about events at home, and he might stroke my hair or pat my thigh. The alarm bells didn't go off until one day, at the end of the appointment without any warning, he cupped my head in his hands, kissed me on the lips, more than once, pulled me into a tight hug, and then pressed his lower body hard against mine. I felt an instant surge of panic and couldn't get out of there fast enough. There was no point in me telling anyone. Who would listen? And more importantly, who would believe me? Uncle Dave was a pillar of the community. That was my last visit.

THE JUDAS' EFFECT

Our family is typical of first-generation Italo-Australian families in that grandparents from both sides were kept close and very much involved in our lives. Parties and huge family dinners were regular memorable events, such as the tradition of quail and polenta hosted by my paternal grandfather (our Nonno) after the opening of each quail season, attended by cousins and more distant relatives. He lived, as did many Italian immigrants of the time in Carlton, known as "Little Italy", on the fringe of Melbourne city. It was a safe, vibrant, community with Italian delis, restaurants, pasticcerias, coffee bars, a movie theatre, and of course a gelateria. People knew each other. They, like our entire family, were hardworking, fun-loving, law-abiding immigrants.

At fourteen, I was still a tomboy in my head even though my body, much to my embarrassment, had already embraced its femininity. One night, as usual after dinner at Nonno's place, my cousins Danny and Leo left to go exploring. They were within a year or two of my age; their dad, Uncle Louie, was my dad's brother, so we saw a lot of each other. That night, they returned and suggested I join them. It was a mild night, dark, but not too late. I was familiar with the neighborhood, having scouted it many times before. My dad's sister, Maria, and her family lived three blocks away in the direction we were heading, and another aunt lived two blocks beyond.

Next to Aunt Maria's place was an older, two-storied apartment building, which she owned and had apartments and rooms to let. Compared to her place, which was painted white and had a green, wrought-iron fence, it seemed a little dreary but not scary. That was until we got inside. The boys suggested we look around. I felt safe entering the building even though I'd never been there, knowing it was next door to my aunt's. In retrospect, that was naïve. My first impression was that it smelled off; so different from the comforting aromas of delicious pasta sauce and espresso coffee that welcomed visitors next door at any time of day. We wandered tentatively around downstairs because not all the hall lights were working, then climbed to the next floor.

As we passed each door, one of them would try the handle to see if it was locked, or perhaps just pretended to, until they arrived at one at the end of the hallway, which was unlocked. They stuck their heads in and said hi to someone beyond my line of sight, then we all crossed the threshold. I was a little nervous, thinking we were trespassing. I remember the lighting was dim, the room claustrophobic, and filled with the smell of something sickly sweet. An older guy, I'd guess to be in his mid-twenties or so, got out of his chair and came towards us. He looked like a vagrant, with unshaven, dirty, matted brown hair, grubby clothes, and yellowing teeth. I was more than surprised that he seemed to be already acquainted with my cousins. I started to feel wary and to wonder what we are doing there.

As I turned to ask them, I was shoved hard from behind, towards their newfound friend. Danny and Leo rushed out; the door slammed shut. For a split second, I froze. I couldn't grasp what was happening as the guy came towards me trying just a bit too hard to be friendly. Turning, I ran for the door, tried the handle, but couldn't get out. Maybe it was jammed. Now I was really frightened and fearing the worst, though I had no specific idea of what form that might take. I just knew that I was feeling threatened. My adrenaline kicked in; I started to run crazily around the room, clambering over the bed, chairs, and whatever else to put some space between us. All the while he was trying to talk me down, suggesting that I might like what he had to offer, and I should at least try it.

The more he kept telling me not to be afraid, the more terrified I became. I didn't scream or yell for help, knowing there was none, but I prayed to God to be rescued. I kept clambering, pleading with him to let me out. After what might have been twenty minutes or so, but felt much longer, his pace slowed, though he continued his attempts to persuade me to be more cooperative. In that conversation, I discovered a deal had been struck with my cousins that he would exchange some dope, apparently their first ever, for a warm body he could have for the evening.

Already in shock, I couldn't bring myself to speak but made another dash for the door. Miraculously it came free, and I escaped, physically unscathed. I ran the few blocks back to Nonno's place, where – no surprise – my cousins were nowhere to be seen. I remained in shock and uncommunicative for weeks, afraid to share the incident with anyone, certain I would be blamed. No doubt my mother dismissed it as me being my usual moody self. When I eventually allowed myself to reflect on the incident, I remembered that I hadn't noticed a key in the door; I'd only seen a lock on the inside, the type that is fixed to the door frame and slides into a fastener behind the door. Even then, I was reluctant to believe the only possible explanation for me being unable to open the door was that one of the cousins was pulling it shut from the outside.

In the following months, the tension between my mother and I escalated to the point that I couldn't bear to be in the same room alone with her. She entered; I'd exit. The reason for her dislike of me was not shared until many years later, which was way too late for it to have changed the course of events. Then, at fifteen, I consciously decided to reject her, spoke only when spoken to, and responded only if it was essential to my own well-being. Meanwhile, my siblings' relationship with her carried on as usual. Whenever she had the chance to criticize or humiliate me in public, she would do so, but always made it sound like she was teasing. As my disappointment and anger grew into rage, with no one to talk to, I sank into a depression, and my exam results tanked. That was beyond distressing.

STEPPING IN FROM THE WINGS

Who should make it known that he was witness to my mother's mistreatment of me, could feel my pain, and see that I needed moral support from someone who cares? None other than Dad's best friend. At first, I couldn't believe it. Finally, someone who I knew, felt safe with, accepted me, and who I had no reason not to trust implicitly. He insisted his new role be our secret because: "It would hurt your dad if he thought I was attempting to take his place."

That made sense. I felt only an overwhelming relief that support was at hand. I could speak openly about my mother, the effect our situation was having on my studies, and anything else that was on my mind. He listened attentively and tried to help me see the situation from my parents' perspective; something I'd never considered before. I felt accepted. My existence was acknowledged favorably, my opinion valued. It was the first time I remember having what I believed to be a real conversation. I looked forward to our secret after-school albeit infrequent meetings with anticipation. I was so grateful for his interest, in truth probably more so, because I enjoyed the warmth of a long hug.

When I first became aware of an alternative motive, I wasn't disturbed by it. It was a subtle change. I almost welcomed it. Having lived so long without physical affection, other than greeting relatives with a meaningless peck on the cheek, his touch was gentle and comforting. I fancied that we had the beginnings of an adult relationship and didn't recognize it for what it was, though was made to see it through a different lens shortly after it ended abruptly months later.

It was reported to the local police by a concerned bystander. As it happened, those officers were regular visitors to Dad's hotel, so they made him aware of their concerns as discreetly as possible to spare him embarrassment. I'm unsure that he was fully aware of the extent of his best friend's betrayal, though I believe that on some level he understood why I might have sought emotional support outside our immediate family. I think it shamed him that he had never addressed the issue of my relationship with my mother. Perhaps he had with her. Not that he ever said. I couldn't bring myself to give him the apology he asked for and was adamant that I would not have turned to his best friend if I didn't feel as unwanted and disconnected from the family. Disappointing to me was that his close friendship with my abuser seemed to continue without much delay or disruption.

Through those potentially more ruinous encounters and the ongoing saga with my mother, the understanding that there is a price to pay for attention, affection, and acceptance became deeply ingrained in my neural pathways as facts of life. But here is where it gets complicated, even confusing. My moods and emotions were all over the shop, had been for years; no doubt due in part to preceding events, as well as the undeniable presence of pubescent hormones that spiked my curiosity about a proper sexual relationship. The distrust which prompted me to keep everyone at arm's length was at odds with my curiosity. Sex was *not* the main event. What I craved was an authentic connection to someone who cared and would have my back. I was still naive enough to think it was possible to find that person and to live the happily-ever-after dream. Nothing else mattered. What I didn't understand was that even if I found such a person, I was completely incapable of connecting to anyone in that same way. Perhaps subconsciously I thought it might happen spontaneously given the right circumstances. If I did, I was dead wrong.

ESCAPE TO MARITAL BLISS

Trapped within the confines of family life in the hotel and adjusting to a new co-ed school, I saw no viable future ahead. Dad had already advised that he would not be funding my plans to attend Melbourne University to study forensic science because: "Italian girls are expected to marry and have children." Based on the available evidence of parental role models, the prospect of marital bliss held no appeal. Far from it. How could I think for a moment that a solution lay there? Until I did. I eloped at age seventeen, only to discover within weeks of the marriage that I had been targeted in the belief my future husband would be invited to join the family hotel business. Why? Because that's what they did back home (his) in Sicily. Not that he had any qualifications or experience that could contribute to it, nor did he have any reason to think he would be welcome. On the few occasions they had all met, Sam didn't leave a good impression. They thought him to be phony. The idea that he might become part of the family was so unlikely in my parents' minds, as to be ludicrous.

As you can imagine, my elopement came as a rude awakening. Dad tracked us down at our city-fringe apartment and offered to forgive my indiscretion and the embarrassment it caused the family if I returned with him to the hotel as if my departure had never happened. Or, if I chose to stay and marry, neither Sam nor I would ever be welcome in his home. No family member would attend the wedding, and I would be cut off from my inheritance. In defiance, I chose the latter. Not the wisest choice I've ever made, for sure. Within a few weeks of our marriage, I came to regret it. Attempts to reconnect to my parents, prompted by Sam against my better judgment, fell on deaf ears. Finally accepting his plan had been stymied, my husband morphed into an outraged, screaming version of Mr. Hyde (of the Dr. Jekyll/Mr. Hyde duo).

From then on, at any time of day or night, I was subjected to regular beatings and pinched, bitten, and forced to dodge whatever projectile he hurled my way. He was determined to beat me into submission. Little did he know. Within minutes of a beating, he would plead for forgiveness with tears streaming, swear never again to lose his temper, and insist on makeup sex. Refusal was not an option. Twenty months later, after a particularly bad beating and many threats to my life, I fled. Knowing he would be after me, I found a job as an au-pair/domestic in a family with two young boys and a baby girl, miles from the city. Even though I had fully explained my situation at the job interview, within six months of starting, I left after the highly principled, previously sympathetic father of the family attempted to take advantage of it.

Though my physical body began to heal, in the months that followed, I ran wild in an attempt to rid myself of the emotional pain. That is, wild for me, who by nature is more introvert than extrovert. I went to nightclubs for the first time, often danced till all hours of the morning, had two or three hours of sleep, and then headed off to work. I fell in with a crowd of Jägermeister-drinking, wiener-schnitzel-eating Germans whose constitution was decidedly more robust than mine. Not a sustainable form of self-medication. At the end of it all, I was thirty pounds heavier, covered from head to toe in angry red hives from alcohol poisoning, and still as miserable as when I began if not more so, which did nothing for my self-image and even less for my self-respect.

Fast-forward through space and time. Underlying themes of manipulation, betrayal, and isolation continued to make their presence felt in both business and personal relationships. By far the saddest and most unexpected betrayal resulted in the loss of my home, a two-bedroom workers' cottage that I had renovated, nestled in a quiet, leafy Brisbane suburb. Let's say that while my professional life surged ahead, my personal life went in the opposite direction. Holding tight to my crippled view of relationships and with no positive expectations, I became conditioned to accept the unacceptable with little consideration for the cost. It was better than nothing. Predictably, there came a time when all coping mechanisms failed. I crashed and could go no further.

If I knew then what I know now, I would have recovered my health sooner. Today, I am aware that everything has a reason and a season, the meaning of karmic consequence, and the spiritual purpose of our existence. I no longer lay the blame for my suffering solely at the feet of my mother, although she was primarily accountable for presenting those lessons in this lifetime. Without them, I would not be the person or the practitioner I am today. To my surprise, I am now profoundly grateful.

ON THE ROAD TO RECOVERY

Of the many sessions I had as an adult with psychologists, psychotherapists, shamans, spiritual gurus, and the like, there were few I recall as defining moments. Following is an overview of one such session, which I hope you find useful.

I attributed the overwhelming sense of inferiority that undermined my life to the belief that I was somehow to blame for my mother's neglect, that I was born genetically flawed, or had committed some unspeakable wrong in infancy. That is until a psychotherapist suggested it might be helpful to examine our family dynamic from a sociological perspective. It was not something that had crossed my mind while trying to make sense of who I was and why I repeatedly made poor choices, so I was intrigued to investigate further.

Using different colored markers, she positioned my family structure, including other people of influence, in a flow-chart on a huge whiteboard. I sat at a distance while she outlined what would be considered normal communication patterns based on our structure, alongside traditional sources of safety and emotional support within it. She included significant events and their aftermath. After hearing about my experiences, she chose a green marker to represent my actual emotional connections, other support mechanisms, and positive communication patterns. It suddenly became crystal clear how my stage had been set for a predictably troubled future, as the scarcity of green markings brought my childhood reality into focus. The core elements that form the building blocks of happy, productive, and healthy interpersonal relationships were mostly absent; those that were there were fragile at best. It was so obvious that I wondered how I hadn't understood it before.

I entered adulthood like a baby giraffe that never found its feet. Did you know that at birth, baby giraffes are dropped from their mother's womb at the height of about eight feet from the ground where they lie almost lifeless, curled up too weak to move? Their mother's role is to kick them into the air, time and again, until they push themselves up onto those long, skinny legs and stretch their torso. They are learning how to recover from a fall and preparing to join the pack; those that don't, become easy prey to leopards and lions. Yet more evidence of truth in nature.

By the end of that session, I had stopped blaming myself for every single poor decision that came before it. Just to be clear, it's not that I opted out of taking responsibility for my own actions; it's that I had a whole new perspective of the subconscious influences that governed them and that had been doing so from childhood. I had been living as a conditioned Self. I remember leaving the psychotherapist's office feeling energized and clear-thinking. In the following days, decades of guilt and blame dissolved from every cell of my body. It was a major turning point on the road to recovery of my self-identity and worth.

DIMENSIONS OF FAMILY BEHAVIOR – COMMUNICATION

What I learned in those sessions was the importance of effective family communication patterns to support healthy emotional growth for all family members. Each member needs to find a communication style that aligns to his or her specific needs, regardless of gender and type of family structure. The family structure in North America is no longer defined as "two parents of opposite gender plus two or three children." Although families have been constitutionally reconfigured due to socio-economic factors and urbanization, the need for connectedness within those structures has not. You may belong to a traditional two-parent family, single-parent family, blended family, stepfamily, or extended family (intergenerational); be fostered or institutionalized; or be raised within an LGBTQ+ family or one of ethnic origin. In all families, members share a commitment to provide each other with emotional, material, and financial support whether the members are bound by blood or legal ties, or live together or apart. Migration from rural to urban environments, overseas job opportunities, and sometimes just simple curiosity to venture farther afield have changed the way we live our lives today. No longer tethered to our village, town, or country of origin, family members can be found spread across the globe, while still accessible and connected.

Connectedness is created in different ways dependent upon cultural norms, though for most, the framework extends beyond verbal expression. Non-verbal behaviors such as facial expressions, presence, eye contact, gestures, and distance or proximity can equally communicate feelings and ideas. Whenever I was in the presence of Nonna, just sitting in the same room in close proximity was comforting, without any need for conversation. Communications can also be symbolic. Many families use hugs, kisses, touch, gifts, special foods, treats, and playfulness to express love and connectedness. Others use silence, withdrawal, offensive gestures, and raised voices to represent anger. These communication patterns educate all family members how to socialize with the external environment and what is appropriate or not in the formation of healthy relationships. In our family, we could tell if Dad had been told of our latest mischief just by looking at his face. And, typical of most European families, food, and lots of it, represented love and connectedness.

DIMENSIONS OF FAMILY BEHAVIOR – COHESION

Sociologists propose we consider two other core concepts of family interaction that have a significant influence on its members' overall well-being and facilitate close communication. The first is "cohesion", defined as emotional bonding through the process of establishing boundaries, creating alliances, spending time together and apart, making friends, developing effective decision-making skills, and enjoying shared activities and recreational time.

Members of balanced, cohesive families tend to experience a seamless blend of emotional independence and closeness to other members, moderate levels of shared activity, respect for family traditions, and a sense of loyalty towards the group. They are supportive of other members and experience genuine feelings of belonging. They live in a co-operative environment. In these families, parents typically adopt a democratic style of parenting, are engaged, encourage open communication, are warm and responsive, set clearly defined rules, are an ongoing source of feedback, and set high expectations.

Studies indicate that children in some, but not all, cultures respond best to this parenting style. They develop a sound self-image, are confident in social situations, achieve higher academic success, enjoy better mental health, and are happier and more independent.

At one extreme of the cohesion spectrum are families in which members are expected to assume high levels of autonomy from an early age, focus on individual rather than shared pursuits, are emotionally separate from other members, and have very little sense of belonging and loyalty. This scenario might reflect parents who are uninvolved or neglectful, have competing priorities and outside interests, have few if any rules, and are reluctant to assume leadership roles. They typically disregard inappropriate behaviors and demonstrate low levels of warmth and affection towards each other as well as their children.

At the opposite end of the cohesion spectrum are families in which there is no independence, members are over-involved in each other's lives, and daily routines are so highly structured as to hamper individual expression and development of each member's unique personal identity. Typically, total loyalty and obedience are demanded, rules are inflexible, and non-compliance results in stern punishment. The meddlesome behavior of helicopter parents is an example of such hyper-parenting. While some could be considered supportive, engaged, and protective parents, through school years and beyond, more controlling ones run interference with every aspect of their children's lives.

Breathing down their necks from a young age, they impose their own ambitions, shield children from the experience of emotional pain, protect them from the consequences of their own actions, discourage independent thinking, and prevent them from making mistakes and failing. Studies from some leading universities have shown that young adults from these families are "more likely to take meds for anxiety and depression… lack social confidence… are less likely to possess the mental strength and discipline needed to achieve personal goals… have poor decision-making skills… demonstrate an inability to manage their emotions appropriately… are more likely to engage in antisocial or violent behaviors." In essence, the development of their True Identity is thwarted.

CASE NOTES   MEET SALLY

Sally is the perfect example of an adult raised in such an environment, as the only female child of three. In her late twenties, she has suffered bouts of depression since her teens, worsened by the sudden death of her dad a few years ago. Always shy of making new connections, she recently decided to take proactive steps to find a life partner. It's not been easy. Sally's mom had been inappropriately sharing details of her marriage with Sally since she turned fifteen. Sally felt obligated to listen. The children were raised in a tightly knit family, the Newman "team", and were taught that what happens in the Newman family, stays within the Newman family. Outsiders cannot be relied upon. Since her father died, Sally and her mom are rarely apart. When Sally isn't at work, her mother too often spends entire weekends in her daughter's apartment.

The few friends she managed to cultivate from work have drifted away, not so keen to pop round for a visit and share intimate details of their personal life with Sally's mom. Dating has proven difficult, mostly because she finds it hard to get close to people and also because her mom finds fault with everyone she brings home. Sally tries to be supportive, understanding her mom's fear of being alone, but all the while she is becoming angrier and more frustrated and overwhelmed. She feels trapped and craves autonomy, but feels guilty for wanting it. I'm pleased to report Sally's transition to her present-day life exceeded beyond expectation. She is enjoying newfound independence, is in a stable relationship, and sees her mom at regular intervals, though not as often.

DIMENSIONS OF FAMILY BEHAVIOR – ADAPTABILITY/FLEXIBILITY

Were you taught as a family member how to respond effectively to crises, change, or other stressors, and how to recover from unexpected or unwanted upheaval? How well do you cope? Sociologists refer to this dimension of family dynamics as "adaptability" or "flexibility". Think of the changes your family has been subject to over time. It may have suffered the loss of a beloved family member, had to contend with serious illness, pregnancy and newborn routines, separation from older children leaving the nest, unexpected caretaking of a grandparent, unplanned redundancy, racism, political instability, or relocation to an unfamiliar community. Any such event uniquely impacts each member. Adaptability relates to the family's capacity to respond to change effectively, restore harmony, and ensure continued stability and cohesion within the group. Along with cohesion, which I prefer to call "closeness", adaptability is a function that needs continuous management for the family to interact effectively. It teaches members how to cope with the ups and downs of life and how to regroup constructively and optimistically. It can only do so through shared, open, respectful communication.

For example, rigid families with strict rules, inflexible structures, and autocratic decision-making, which stifle emotional expression between its members, typically find it difficult to adapt successfully to change. New routines are a major disruption as they pose the threat of parental loss of control, so these families tend to repress change. The consequences I have seen first-hand relate to clients whose parents adhered strictly to the rigorous demands of extreme cultural or religious ideologies, and others with at least one parent and a family history within the armed forces. Those clients were required to follow in their parents' footsteps unwaveringly, with any curiosity about an independent lifestyle discouraged, to safeguard the sanctity of the family unit.

The other end of the flexibility continuum is the chaotic family, which has no apparent leadership structure, inconsistent or no rules and guidelines, permissive parents, low expectations of its members, and regular experiences of upheaval. Parents may be regularly unemployed, chemical or alcohol dependent, suffer mental illness or be abusive, and be neglectful of family members' basic physical and emotional needs. Those circumstances expose all family members to vulnerability, potential trauma, and an unpredictable and sometimes frightening environment. Often deprived of the experience of being loved and accepted unconditionally, these children move through their teen years to adulthood feeling disconnected, unworthy, shameful, unimportant, highly stressed, unlovable, and fearful of the outside world. Frequently being witness to parents numbing their feelings with all kinds of addictions, they have no sense of how to safely and constructively express emotion or to form healthy friendships and more intimate relationships. With no learned coping mechanisms, many succumb themselves to the maladaptive or antisocial behaviors of their parents or end up on the streets.

That being said, it is important to recognize that social issues such as poverty, ethnic cultural norms and expectations, and broader societal values also play a role in a family's capacity to adapt to change. If income is inconsistent, the family is comprised of one parent, or relies solely on social welfare, change and upheaval serve only to increase stress levels and instability. It's not to say that every family dynamic falls into these specific categories. However, it is proven that malfunctioning families typically produce malfunctioning children whose future is impaired by self-destructive beliefs, attitudes, and behaviors learned in early childhood. Understanding how your family dynamic has shaped your present reality can help relieve the burden of shame and self-blame. It means you no longer need to be held hostage by your past choices. Take your time to reflect on both your past and present family dynamic. Be patient. Be courageous enough to probe deeply to discover the true cause of your dissatisfaction or unhappiness, and you will be well rewarded.

EXERCISE: RECLAIM YOUR TRUE IDENTITY AND SELF-ESTEEM

- Take the time to review your life, within the context of events such as I have done. Document those defining moments and events, reducing the narrative for each one to bullet point format. This step will help you reconnect with any feelings you have suppressed over time, clarify your thoughts, provide much-needed perspective, and relieve you of the misconception that you are solely to blame for everything that has since happened.

- If your head and heart are feeling cluttered, I recommend you return to Chapter 6, Accessing Your Creative Genius, before you go further. The guidelines and simple exercises there will best prepare you to move forward.
- This next step frees you from the pain of corrosive emotions and unhappy memories. The Inventory of Corrosive Emotions and Attributes associated with Loss of Identity and Self-esteem, which follows, will help you identify those. Write them down, and allocate a numeric rating from 0-10, using the guidelines in Chapter 7. Process each one that applies using the script for Release of Corrosive Emotions that follows as an example. It's easy to personalize the underlined part of the script to suit your own needs, though it's important to keep it short and on point.
- NOTE: If you are feeling resistant, it could be that you are being sabotaged by subconscious resistance, which is fear-based. Refer to Chapter 8, which contains beliefs specific to resistance and stagnation. Weed those out before returning to this page.
- Self-forgiveness is key to laying a new foundation. Stop beating yourself up. Once you have rid yourself of the trauma and other negative emotions, you will feel much lighter, freer, and optimistic and capable of moving forward with positive momentum. Readers who have suffered too much for too long may still be carrying the weighty burden of self-blame. If you are one of those, the Self-Forgiveness Script is a critical, non-negotiable element on your road to recovery. It can be found in Chapter 8.

RELEASE OF CORROSIVE EMOTIONS

I acknowledge my feelings of <u>hopelessness as an impediment to my Life goals</u>, so now release them from their earliest point of origin, from every aspect of my life and across all dimensions of time. I am supported by the Universe in this choice.

IDENTITY AND SELF-ESTEEM
CORROSIVE EMOTIONS & ATTRIBUTES

Abandoned	Failure	Rejected
Angry	Frightened	Repressed
Anxious	Frustrated	Ruined
Baffled	Grief	Sad
Betrayed	Guilt	Second-Rate
Chaotic	Helpless	Shame
Confused	Hopelessness	Skeptical
Critical	Ignored	Stagnant
Crushed	Impatient	Stumped
Defeated	Impotent	Subdued
Depressed	Inadequate	Suspect
Deprived	Inferior	Suspicious
Desperate	Insecure	Trapped
Destitute	Invisible	Unacknowledged
Directionless	Isolated	Undeserving
Disconnected	Judgmental	Unfriendly
Disempowered	Lonely	Ungrounded
Disgusted	Lost	Unlovable
Disheartened	Manipulated	Unloved
Disorganized	Mean	Unsafe
Disrespected	Miserly	Unworthy
Distrusting	Misunderstood	Victimized
Embarrassment	Muddle-headed	Withholding
Exhausted	Neglected	Wounded

RECLAIM YOUR IDENTITY AND SELF-ESTEEM

EXERCISE: SELF-DEFEATING BELIEFS AND MISCONCEPTIONS

Emerge from the confusion of limiting beliefs. The fact is that *any* circumstance that causes us to live unhappily compromises our integrity and freedom of expression, crushes our spirit, and diminishes any chance we have of a fulfilling life. We become distanced from our empowered Self, clouded by a distorted view of reality.

- Most important: please take your time with the process. Find a quiet place to be, where you are unlikely to be interrupted. Relax, take regular breaths. Slowly, read each belief to yourself at least twice, so you start to get a feel for which beliefs are true for you. Be kind to yourself on the path to recovery; healing is a journey, not a transaction.
- Following is a comprehensive Inventory of Self-Defeating Beliefs and Misconceptions being fed to you by that annoying, persistent voice in your head. It's so easy to reprogram your thoughts and beliefs once you have let go of the emotions that anchor them.
- Identify those beliefs most closely aligned to your personal experience, then release them using the script for Release of Self-Defeating Beliefs I've included below the Inventory. No doubt you have other unhelpful thoughts and attitudes that need fixing. There's no limit to what you can do with these scripts. Go for it!

IDENTITY AND SELF-ESTEEM
SELF-DEFEATING BELIEFS

- Change is difficult.
- Change mostly brings unwanted consequences.
- Healing and change are possible for others, but not for me.
- I am trapped in my situation.
- I am powerless to make changes.
- I have no control over my life.
- Bad things keep happening to me.
- It's my fault.
- It's hard to let go of the past.
- No one can help me.
- People don't like me.
- People always judge me.
- People don't understand me.
- No one sees the real me.
- People don't listen to me.
- My opinions don't matter.
- If I tell people how I feel, they'll think I'm crazy or being ridiculous.
- Most people can't be trusted.
- Most people lie.
- I am unlovable.
- I am worthless.
- I don't deserve a happy life, successful career, or a loving partner.
- I am a loser (a failure).
- I am stupid.

RECLAIM YOUR IDENTITY AND SELF-ESTEEM

- I often feel I am incompetent.
- I often feel I am flawed.
- I'm not good enough.
- I can't do anything right.
- I don't fit in anywhere.
- I hate myself and my life.
- Life isn't fair.
- I wish I had someone else's life.
- I always draw the short straw.
- I'm the unluckiest person I know.
- Relationships don't work.
- Relationships are too much work.
- Relationships are stifling.
- Relationships mean deprivation of independence.
- People I love always leave me.
- No one would like me when they got to know me.
- I make people angry.
- It is always better to say nothing than to say what I really feel.
- Talking about how you feel creates trouble.
- I am bound to be rejected.
- I'll always be alone.
- The world around me is not a safe place.
- I am unsupported by the Universe/God.

RELEASE OF SELF-DEFEATING BELIEFS

The concept that <u>it sounds too simple to actually work</u> no longer serves my best interests. I release it now from every cell of my body, every aspect of my life, and across all dimensions of time. I am supported by the Universe in this transition.

The previous steps incorporate all the essential elements of the entire program to clear a path for the True Self to re-emerge. I've had amazing feedback from so many whose lives have been transformed simply by working through the weeding scripts. You too can join them in feeling much happier, more confident, freer, and in control of a newfound direction. No longer emotionally triggered by certain people or circumstances, they are living as creative, expressive, and joyful beings.

BONUS: SUPERCHARGED CREATIVE DOWNLOAD SCRIPTS

- Sprinkle some stardust on your newfound Self! Creative Downloads are most effective when you've processed the worst of your corrosive emotions and misguided beliefs.
- In Chapter 7, you discovered the Inventory of Life-Affirming Choices, which reflects only feel-good emotions and attributes to which you might aspire. In Chapter 8, you will find the Script for Creative Downloads to replace misguided beliefs and attitudes, which work in the same way. Adding both to your toolbox will be like reprogramming your new reality on steroids. Enjoy!

Chapter 10

No More Secrets: Surviving the Aftermath of Abuse

Abuse can alter the direction of your life irreversibly if you allow it. The worst damage of abuse in all its forms is not physical; it's the indelible psychological and emotional imprint, which takes much longer to heal and has you convinced you have no better option. I've been there, done that. Some victims never heal. You may think you are coping by keeping regular routines on an even keel and accommodating your abuser's needs. From personal experience, I can reassure you, you're not. The purpose of this chapter is to help you process the emotional and psychological effects of abuse safely and effectively and to help you rebuild a life that is creative, expressive, loving, and fulfilling. You can see from my own story, and from those of clients whose stories I share here, that such a life is possible.

The context in which we refer to abuse has changed significantly over the past three decades and is recognized today on a global scale as a serious social problem. Its scope has also been redefined. Rather than being commonly associated with overt behaviors such as rape and sexual assault, or its consequences as black eyes, bruises, and broken bones, it is now examined through a broader lens. Those changes have been brought about in part as a response to increased public outcry and the introduction of long-overdue amendments to family law and criminal law in most Western countries.

In the US, in addition to the physical and sexual harm inflicted by a spouse or intimate partner, the term abuse encompasses emotional, psychological, financial/economic, cultural, elder maltreatment and exploitation, neglect, child abuse, and stalking. Statistically, women are the subject of all forms of abuse far more frequently than men, though men are now reporting incidents of abuse by women in growing numbers. The types of abuse commonly inflicted by women upon men, which cause the least physical harm range from criticism, ridicule, and harassment; throwing things; deprivation of sex and affection; threats to harm children or pets; and damage to personal items of value. The degree of cruelty escalates over time to more violent behaviors such as punching, kicking, biting, and assault using a gun, knife, or another object to cause physical harm. A major differentiating factor in the reported incidents of abuse across all gender identities is that men are less likely to report than women. For many male victims, incidents go unreported due to potential embarrassment or shame, the woman's threats to ensure the victim is separated from their children, and the belief expressed by many male victims that the "system works against them."

Surveys of both male and female victims of intimate partner violence reveal that a pattern of emotional and verbal abuse exists for years, sometimes decades before interactions become violent, and that those behaviors almost always precede physical abuse, which goes unreported until the violence escalates. If you are unsure if you are a victim of verbal abuse, there's a book that will help you clarify your situation. *The Verbally Abusive Relationship: How to Recognize It and How to Respond* (third edition) by Patricia Evans, an internationally acclaimed interpersonal communications specialist and bestselling author, is one of the most powerful books on the subject. Ms. Evans single-handedly brought the subject of verbal abuse to the forefront of American consciousness as a guest on more than two hundred radio programs and seventeen national TV programs, including the *Oprah Winfrey Show*, *Sonya Live – CNN*, and *News Talk*. Her website is listed in the Resources pages in this book.

In its earliest stages, abusers' behaviors can be so subtle as to be unrecognizable. Their goal is to acquire dominance and control over their victim, typically through the use of tactics such as intimidation, isolation, humiliation, denial, and blame. Survivors often blame themselves for missing the signs, though of course they are not to blame, nor could they have changed the course of events. It's unlikely it entered their mind that they were being manipulated and deceived, or that they would ever be held captive by emotional abuse or violence, when they first met their charming, smart, and persuasive date; at their engagement; or even in the early days of marriage. It is difficult to seriously consider you are being abused when your abuser's behaviors are masked by honey-sweet tones, overt displays of thoughtfulness, cooperation, financial support, or romantic gestures. Those seemingly normal behaviors are merely bait to keep you hooked into that relationship.

A disturbing case that comes immediately to mind is a client who was swept off her feet by an attentive, generous new boyfriend, and enticed to a "really romantic long weekend getaway." In fact, she was abducted, taken to a remote cabin in the woods and subjected to all manner of abuse for almost six months. She was surprised that he returned her to the city alive, albeit under threat if she reported it. She did, and he was later charged.

Abuse does not discriminate. Patterns of abuse can occur within any age group; across gender identities; within all cultures, religious groups, and socio-economic backgrounds; in homes, the workplace, at schools, in hospitals, welfare institutions, and aged-care facilities; and increasingly through social media and cell phone. Abuse has long-term rippling effects. Studies have shown that women subjected to sexual, emotional, and physical abuse in childhood experience significantly worse overall health in adulthood than women who have not been abused. Abused women have higher rates of hospitalization for illness and suffer more long-term physical and mental health challenges, including: post-traumatic stress syndrome, higher levels of anxiety, eating disorders, chronic digestive issues, insomnia, alcohol and drug abuse, depression, and suicidal tendencies. Childhood abuse also increases the likelihood of abuse in adulthood.

The following stories are typical of many abused clients that have passed through my door who are now living their life of choice.

CASE NOTES   MEET KATIE

Katie is a guidance counselor, esteemed for her compassionate nature. Born to devout Christian parents, she was taught to be considerate, attentive, and obedient from an early age with the promise that those qualities would ensure a happy, long-lasting marriage. Within a few years of her marriage to the person everyone believed was a "perfect match", she found herself trapped in a relationship she was ill-equipped to manage.

"He was quite popular in our congregation, always prepared to lend a helping hand to anyone in need, and active in the men's church maintenance crew. I hadn't been looking for a partner, so was surprised and elated when he started to pay me attention. It helped that he was charismatic, intelligent, and easy on the eye. I was flattered that he chose me. As it turns out, he had had me in his sights for a while.

"Thinking back on the marriage, I can see when he started to subtly manipulate what I was doing, where I was going, who I could and couldn't spend time with away from home. He quizzed me on who called when he was at work and why. At the time, I was working part-time and pregnant with our first child, so didn't pay much attention to it. Not too long after the baby arrived, I became aware that he had transitioned from a friendly, sociable, occasional drinker to something else. The more he drank, the more belittling he would be. It only really pushed my buttons when he started to criticize my family and friends, who had been nothing but kind and loving towards him.

"Privately he found fault with just about everything I did, from the meals we shared, my clothes, to the attention I was giving to my firstborn. For years I blamed myself, thinking that perhaps I wasn't a good wife, that my expectations of marriage might be unrealistic. I had never seen my parents be anything other than supportive and caring towards each other, so assumed that was how it was going to be for me, too. When he was home, I was walking on eggshells, never knowing what might happen next. I had become used to the constant stream of insults, name calling, stuff being thrown about, and doors slamming. I worried about the effect he was having on the children who were now both old enough to understand what was going on. What would be best for them? As time passed, I became more fragile and confused, lost my sense of self, and felt defeated. I was raised to be accommodating, and the thought of talking to Mom or my friends about my doubts was embarrassing. Fear that he would find out and retaliate also played into my decision not to speak out.

"The day came that forced me to rethink the idea that my situation could change without any external intervention. It was a rainy Saturday, so the children were unable to play outside. They were good kids, never really noisy, but that day they were arguing over the TV remote. He lost it and went into a rage. What had in the past been the odd "accidental" shove or slap suddenly became a full-on physical attack, punching, pinching, screaming, and shoving me to the floor, blaming me for the kids' disagreement. They were shocked by the attack, but afraid and helpless to do anything. Seeing their fear and hurt at that moment was the catalyst I needed. On Monday, I spoke to Mom and Dad, who were not as surprised as I thought they would be. They had noticed how much I'd changed since the marriage, though were reluctant to interfere, not knowing how bad my situation was.

"In the following days, I went to the police, contacted a women's shelter on the far side of town, and made plans to leave. He came home from work one day; we were gone. I know I made the right decision; the only decision that I could have made. I won't say the transition to our new life was a breeze; the first few years we all lived in fear that he would find us. The children and I now live in a different state. We are happy, more relaxed, and settled with new friends and a supportive community. The children are safe and doing well at school. I am not the person I was before the marriage, and glad of it. Thanks to you, I'm more independent, decisive, courageous and opinionated – in a good way."

CASE NOTES   MEET JODI

Jodi was a fiercely independent, well-traveled interior design consultant at the time she married in her late twenties. She loved socializing and meeting new people, but figured it was time to settle down to raise a family. Her choice of partner was close to her own age, equally hard-working but far less traveled. Nor was he as inclined to socialize much outside his immediate family. He intrigued her. She'd always drifted towards the "dark, silent, broody type" with reasonable success in the past.

"Given my age, when we married, we decided to start a family right away. Within five years, we had two boys and a girl, and I loved being a mom. Keeping me housebound suited my husband's purpose, although I wasn't aware of it then. When we were dating, there had been a few red flags I missed. With my heart set on marrying as soon as I could when I got back from Europe, I started dating again, but he was the first one I really liked, and the sexual chemistry kept me coming back for more.

"He would ask about my travels and past boyfriends, and I felt it only right to share, without going into too much detail. More often than not, his response was to make mean remarks, in sort of a jokey way. I laughed them off, thinking he was cute and just a little bit jealous. Other times, after those conversations he would get moody and withdrawn and wouldn't speak for hours, or sometimes all day. It didn't occur to me then that he was controlling and manipulative. Whenever I suggested it was his turn to share, he wasn't as open, was evasive, or would infer he had had limited experience with women. On some level, I found that believable because of his moodiness. Years later, one of his brothers let the cat out of the bag, assuming I already knew. ("He had a string of girlfriends before you. They didn't last long; he's so picky.")

"I also thought it odd that he never introduced me to his friends, the few he supposedly had, but maybe he thought I wouldn't like them. It didn't occur to me that he felt threatened by the thought of me meeting them. In retrospect, I see that my impatience to settle down blinded me and prevented me from asking more questions and insisting on answers. Regardless, all I could see was us as a "cute couple". I desperately wanted a long-term relationship, so when he asked me to go exclusive after only two months or so, I gave in, thinking, *How romantic is that?* In truth, a small part of me felt cautious; I should have listened to my gut. I told Mom years later that I remember hearing her voice in my ear, saying: 'Marry in haste, repent at leisure.'

"When our youngest was five, I decided to go back to work part-time. I missed my independence and having adult conversations and somewhere else to go. He didn't take that too well. Feeling that he was losing control, his moodiness and frustration escalated. He accused me of wanting to have relationships with other men and that it was the real reason I wanted to be away from home. I went anyway. At home, he was critical and suspicious of what I might be doing when we were not together. While I was at work, he called incessantly, which was noted and frowned upon. I became so embarrassed and frustrated by the disruption that I eventually gave it up and decided to see clients from home.

"Fast forward to now. The children are in their teens. As far as dads go, he hasn't been the worst. He has never hurt them or me physically, but the constant moodiness, belittling, criticism, and arguments have drained us all emotionally and physically, even though I have tried to protect the children as much as I could. One of the boys idolizes his dad, and I'm sad to say, follows in his footsteps as far as verbal abuse towards me and his brother and sister. His behavior has been reported at school, he's not well-liked, and his grades aren't all that impressive. My other son and my daughter worry for me and are as protective as they can be in the circumstances. They are both doing well academically and socially.

"A few years ago, I shared my secret with parents and friends, who have all been extremely supportive, even though they don't understand why I'm still there. Of course, the thought of leaving has crossed my mind many times, but I made the decision when the children were young that I'd persevere for their sakes. Although, if the abuse had become physical, I don't think I would have stayed. The only thing I've ever wanted was for them to have a stable home, a quality of life, and the opportunities that having two incomes can provide. They go to good schools, and I've insisted they attend as many school social events and sporting activities as they want. Two of the three are well adjusted, compassionate young adults, I'm proud of them. I think it was worth the sacrifice."

Jodi came to see me hoping to recover what she referred to as her "emotional immunity." She was at her lowest ebb. Though resigned to stay in the marriage for practical reasons, she admitted she hadn't been coping with the stress and uncertainty of it for many years. When things were good between her and her husband, and he was quieter and less critical, she was always waiting for the other shoe to drop. Over the years, she'd not only lost the independence she so highly valued, but she'd completely lost her sense of self. She often wondered what happened to the funny, spontaneous, happy person she had been.

We put together a simple plan to recover those and other attributes Jodi needed and to realign her beliefs about what she thought could be possible going forward in that relationship. They are still together. She has recovered her voice, is now living a life within a life, has coffee with newfound friends, and has recently joined a local group of outdoor enthusiasts who meet up every weekend. She reports that her husband has "mellowed" and that at some point, he realized it was either that or a costly, embarrassing divorce.

CASE NOTES   **MEET MELANIE**

Melanie was a happy, intelligent, twenty-seven-year-old, who was employed by a high-end ad agency as a receptionist/admin assistant when she was raped by a fellow employee. She blamed herself because she'd been drinking and kept it a secret from friends and family because she was too embarrassed and ashamed. She also decided not to report the attack to law enforcement. Due to the emotional and psychological challenges she's experienced since then, she shared her story for the first time with me, five years on.

Since starting college, her heart was set on leaving home for the big city, finding someone to share a flat with, and landing a job in the advertising industry. It didn't matter that she would have to start at the bottom rung; it was where she was meant to be. After many rejected applications, she finally landed a job in one of the largest downtown agencies. Melanie found a cute but compact apartment with stunning views not too far away. It was an optimistic start to her new life. Quick to learn, attractive, and helpful, she soon caught the eye of one of the younger account execs. He seemed to hover more than necessary at the front desk where she spent her day and often sought her out when she was in the breakroom. Quickly smitten and overwhelmed by his attention, Melanie started fantasizing about their connection as something other than what it was.

One evening after staff drinks in the office, a few employees including Melanie and her "prospective boyfriend" drifted off to a local bar. She had been drinking steadily but felt she was more sober than not when he invited her back to his apartment and the potential relationship took a turn for the worst. She remembers feeling woozy, disoriented, and no longer in control. After raping her repeatedly, he threatened to spread the word among the other execs that she was "up for it" if she reported him to anyone at work or to law enforcement. Still in shock and afraid of retaliation, after a few days off work, she continued as though nothing had happened. On her visits home, her family noticed a significant change in her self-confidence and usually happy disposition. They were all worried but put it down to the pressures of working downtown in a busy ad agency and their belief that Melanie had been enjoying an active social life.

Since the assault, Melanie has become increasingly anxious, not been sleeping well, lost her appetite and weight she can ill-afford to lose, and no longer feels safe. She feels angry, worthless, and stupid for not recognizing the perpetrator's manipulation for what it was – just as he intended and had done so many times before. She refuses to go out without her girlfriends and has not been on a date for years. She slips into a victim mindset anytime she is around a man other than her dad or her brother. The flashbacks and nightmares are still happening. Although she has no regrets about not reporting the assault, she now recognizes the need to process the incident properly. Living in denial and fear has been eating away at her. What made it worse was a somewhat irrational decision to stay in the job because she was excited about her recent move to a creative role where she was making her presence felt. That had always been the goal.

To start the process of healing, my goal was to recover Melanie's self-esteem and confidence by releasing cellular shock and trauma from the initial incident, and then the fears and misconceptions that had risen as a consequence. She made good progress relatively quickly. Then, despite her initial reluctance, Melanie agreed that it would be in her best interests to find alternative employment. Her abuser was also still employed there and had risen in rank to a more senior role, albeit not in close physical proximity. The last I heard, Melanie is very happily making her presence felt elsewhere in the advertising scene, is dating and socializing, and has returned to her "old self", though much the wiser.

Each of these clients managed their abuser and the consequence of their abuse in a different way, dependent upon the degree of threat or nature of the abuse, whether they had dependent children, their own emotional capacities, and their aspirations for the future. There is no one-size-fits-all solution. Whether you have left the abusive relationship or stayed as Jodi did to live "a life within a life", the following steps to recovery will help you regain your sense of self and courage to move forward. Don't forget to be patient and kind to yourself as you unravel the aftermath of your abuse.

EXERCISE: RECOVERING FROM THE AFTERMATH OF ABUSE

It is important to acknowledge that some of the emotions and attitudes contributing to your current state of distress or confusion may have been pre-existing, causing you to be vulnerable. Being able to define those is pertinent to your recovery.

- Take stock of your life, mindfully, within the context of events such as I have done in the previous chapter – Reclaim Your Identity and Self-Esteem. This step will help you reconnect with any feelings you have suppressed over time, clarify your thoughts, provide much-needed perspective, and relieve you of the misconception that you are solely to blame for everything that has since happened.
- Most important: please take your time with the process. Find a quiet place to be, where you are unlikely to be interrupted. Relax, take regular breaths. Slowly, read each element of the inventories at least twice to get a feel for which beliefs are true for you. Be kind to yourself; healing is a journey, not a transaction.
- If your head and heart are feeling cluttered, I recommend you return to Chapter 6, Accessing Your Creative Genius, before you go further. The guidelines and simple exercises there will best prepare you to move forward.
- Free yourself from corrosive emotions and unhappy memories. The following inventory of Corrosive Emotions and Attributes shared by victims of abuse will help you identify those. Write them down, and allocate a numeric rating from 0-10, using the guidelines in Chapter 7. If you feel a little

overwhelmed by the prospect of releasing those emotions, it could be that you are being sabotaged by subconscious resistance, which is fear-based. Refer to Chapter 8, which contains beliefs specific to resistance and stagnation. Process those before returning to your list.

RECOVERING FROM ABUSE
CORROSIVE EMOTIONS & ATTRIBUTES

Abandoned	Frightened	Pessimistic
Angry	Frustrated	Regretful
Anxious	Grief/Loss	Rejected
Betrayed	Guilt	Repressed
Bored	Hostile	Resentful
Confused	Impressionable	Restrained
Crushed	Inadequate	Sad
Defeated	Incompetent	Second-rate
Dejected	Inferior	Shameful
Demoralized	Insecure	Threatened
Depressed	Intimidated	Trapped
Deprived	Isolated	Undermined
Desperate	Lonely	Unlovable
Directionless	Manipulated	Unloved
Disappointed	Marginalized	Unsafe
Disconnected	Misunderstood	Victimized
Disempowered	Muted	Violent
Disrespected	Needy	Vulnerable
Embarrassed	Numb	Weak
Exhausted	Outraged	Worthless
Frantic	Overwhelmed	Wounded

As you move forward with your recovery, don't forget to practice self-forgiveness. Stop beating yourself up. If you have suffered too much for too long, you are probably carrying the weighty burden of self-blame. If so, the Self-Forgiveness Script in chapter 8 is a critical, non-negotiable step of your healing journey.

RELEASE OF CORROSIVE EMOTIONS

I acknowledge my feelings of <u>being defeated as an impediment to my goals of Family and Relationship</u>, so now release them from their earliest point of origin, from every aspect of my life and across all dimensions of time. I am supported by the Universe in this choice.

Reprogram your beliefs and self-perception. Any circumstance that causes us to live unhappily compromises our integrity and freedom of expression. Distanced from our True Self, we develop a distorted view of reality. Following is the Inventory of Self-Defeating Beliefs and Misconceptions also compiled from client histories and my own experiences. I am delighted to share that we are all now fully recovered and surrounded by healthy, supportive relationships. I suggest you use these beliefs as a starting point and then add whatever comes to mind.

RECOVERING FROM ABUSE
SELF-DEFEATING BELIEFS

- Change is difficult for me.
- Change mostly brings unwanted consequences.
- Healing and change are possible for others, but not for me.
- I am trapped in my situation.
- I am powerless to make change.
- I have no control over my life.
- No one can help me.
- I don't have the courage or the mental stamina to push through this crisis.
- I am not a resourceful person.
- I am to blame for his/her abuse.
- It's not his/her fault that he/she is an abuser.
- I don't know who I am without a husband/wife/lover/partner.
- I don't know what I want. I am confused.
- I am afraid of what my future might look like.
- I'm just not good on my own.
- This relationship is better than nothing.
- Better the devil you know, than the one you don't.
- Maybe I'm just not seeing this situation clearly.
- Maybe I'm not flexible enough.
- Maybe I complain too much.
- I take things too seriously. (He/she always tells me that.)
- I'm overly sensitive. I over-react.
- I make people angry.

- His/her needs are more important than my own.
- My children's/my parents'/others' needs are more important than my own.
- To be a good wife/husband/mother/father/daughter/son, I need to sacrifice my own needs and wants.
- It is not useful to have boundaries.
- There is always a cost to saying "no".
- Saying "no" is never the right thing to do/the Christian thing to do.
- Most men/women cannot be trusted.
- Most men/women are liars.
- I don't fit in anywhere.
- Life is an uphill battle.
- Relationships don't work.
- Relationships are too much work.
- Relationships mean abuse.
- Relationships are stifling.
- Relationships mean deprivation of independence.
- It is always better to say nothing than to say what I really feel.
- Speaking my truth always brings trouble/unwanted consequences.
- I'll always be alone.
- The world around me is not a safe place.
- I am unsupported by the Universe/God.

The previous steps incorporate all the essential elements of the entire program to clear a path for the True Self to re-emerge. I've had amazing feedback from so many students and clients whose lives have been transformed simply by working through the weeding scripts. You too can join them in feeling much happier, more confident, freer, and in control of a newfound direction. No longer emotionally triggered by certain people or circumstances, they are living as creative, expressive, and joyful beings.

BONUS: SUPERCHARGED CREATIVE DOWNLOAD SCRIPTS

- Sprinkle some stardust on your newfound Self! Remember that Creative Downloads are most effective when you've processed the worst of your corrosive emotions and misguided beliefs.
- In Chapter 7, you discovered the Inventory of Life-Affirming Choices, which reflects only feel-good emotions and attributes to which you might aspire. In Chapter 8, you will find the Script for Creative Downloads to replace misguided beliefs and attitudes, which work in the same way. Adding both to your toolbox will be like reprogramming your new reality on steroids. Enjoy!

Chapter 11

De-Mystifying Eating Disorders and Weight Loss

According to some of the top US researchers in the field of eating disorders, associated with the University of Minnesota Medical School, currently over 30 million people in the US alone suffer from eating disorders. Another study, published in the *American Journal of Psychiatry* reveals that people with eating disorders have the highest mortality rate of all those suffering from mental illness. We now know that eating disorders and a preoccupation with weight and body image have little to do with food and everything to do with the beliefs and emotions that undermine healthy self-esteem. Those disorders are coping mechanisms, which become addictions in the same way as opioids, alcohol, cigarettes, sex, and self-harm. They all represent an external manifestation of internal distress, and feelings of being overwhelmed with no way out. An addict's compulsive behavior is a misguided attempt to control otherwise unmanageable circumstances, while unquestionably seeking a mood change, such as the calming effect associated with elevated levels of serotonin. Attempts by those with eating disorders to find relief by bingeing and purging, extreme self-discipline, excessive exercise, abuse of diet pills and laxatives, self-punishment, and eating to excess provide only momentary comfort and a distorted sense of control. All things considered, based on the report published in the *American Journal of Psychiatry*, it is clear those methods are unsuccessful.

In my experience, the root cause of most addiction can be traced to a past trauma or transformative events that have led to profound feelings of shame, guilt, and low self-esteem that the addict is unable to process. They become disillusioned, subject to depression, and may have irrational beliefs and suicidal thoughts. In fact, I believe that *all* dysfunction, other than the "less than 5% inheritable disease" discovered by epigenetic scientists, stems from an inability to identify, express, and properly process corrosive emotions and confounded thinking. Both clients in private consultation and participants from past workshops, who were kind enough to share their stories, have tracked the onset of their eating disorder to one or more of the following points of origin:

- Relationship conflict (current or past)
- Fears (rational or unfounded)
- Traumatic event (death or loss of someone close)
- Boredom
- Loneliness (wanting to be accepted, liked)
- Depression due directly to low self-esteem
- Being overwhelmed by tight or restrictive schedules (lack of self-care, self-sacrifice)
- Being ignored

- Being abused, bullied, belittled, or manipulated
- Inability to identify and express emotions appropriately
- Earlier deprivation of food

Many of those who contributed their story had never made the connection between these unhappy circumstances and the changes in their eating habits even though they were adults who had been suffering for years, some for decades. Others who had attended counseling were managing better, although were still plagued by negative self-beliefs, poor self-image, and emotional distress. Before you continue through the five-steps to recovery, here are a few stories that give you some insight into what is possible.

CASE NOTES — MEET KRISTINA

Kristina had been to counselors, psychologists, and other practitioners for years before she found her way to my office. Married at almost thirty, much later than her sisters, she now has two daughters and loves being a mom. Her husband is self-employed as an event organizer and doing well. The idea that she had a serious problem didn't dawn on Kristina until her mid-twenties, when a friend put a label to it. She suggested that Kristina's morbid fear of weight gain, accompanied by all-too-frequent trips to the washroom immediately after a meal, compulsive exercising, and overuse of diuretics and laxatives were known symptoms of bulimia. Kristina argued that she wasn't bulimic, her binge-eating and purging were just a way of managing her weight, something she'd learned as a teen. At first sight, if you ignored her skeletal appearance, she looked amazing sporting the latest fashion trends, always tanned, her hair and makeup done perfectly; she could be any one of the androgynous models you would find in the pages of *Vogue*, *Elle*, or *Harper's Bazaar*.

She had been hiding her shameful secret for decades from her family, friends, and her husband. It took no time at all to discover the root cause of the problem. Since early childhood, she had been unfavorably compared to her elder sister, Isabella, who was closest to Kristina in age. Isabella was striking, even as a young child; she was spirited, adventurous, and willful and everybody's favorite. Equally intelligent, Kristina was the quieter–plain-faced, studious, obedient, and accommodating. In fact, she was over-accommodating, in an unsuccessful attempt to win her parents' approval. They made no effort from the outset to share their affection equally between the three siblings. Isabella was always front and center of their attention and got whatever she asked of her parents.

All three were provided a university education, enjoyed an active social life, and went on to hold responsible positions within their respective field of endeavor. When at university, if Kristina happened to introduce any of her male friends to Isabella, they almost all drifted in Isabella's direction; few remained loyal. Those lessons were painful, so she made a conscious effort to lead an independent social life. She still does.

Opportunities for Kristina to secretly eat a huge bag of candies in one sitting or to enjoy a proper family meal and then rush to the washroom to purge are now limited. Her two daughters have recently reached an age where they notice, and they voice their concern about anything out of the ordinary, which is why Kristina came to me, seeking a permanent solution to this complication in her life. Even though she knows without reservation that her husband loves her, she worries about how he would react if he ever discovered her secret. My guess was that he already knew. How could he not? Also, expectedly, after so many years of deprivation, her addictive behavior has taken its toll on her body, despite regular intravenous injections of vitamins and minerals, and other wholesome additions to her daily routine. She is now consulting with a naturopath and has committed to continue beyond the scope of our sessions.

Within only five sessions, Kristina was totally relieved of the emotional burden and distorted beliefs supporting her addiction. She has regained her freedom and is eating normally. You can, too.

CASE NOTES **MEET HELEN**

Helen's mom is an Advanced Practice Registered Nurse (APRN) in one of the largest hospitals in the state. She also takes a broader view of physical health as it connects to the mind and spirit, which is why she came to be sitting in front of me, worried about her daughter. "Helen is a bright, honest, outgoing, and reliable daughter; the best I could ever hope for. She has a great group of friends, girls and boys, most of which I've met and like – some she's had since grade school. She gets good grades and likes to study. When she was fourteen, her dad left us and has since remarried. Although they are in a good place now, she didn't want to see him for a few years after the split. A little while after her sixteenth birthday, she seemed to become suddenly distant and much less communicative, which was so unlike her, because since her dad left, we have become even closer than we were before. She's always shared her day-to-day news spontaneously. It's never been like pulling teeth, even though I'm her mom. She's that sort of girl. But that isn't who she is now.

"The reason I've come to see you is that Helen has become very ill. She is addicted to soda, drinks at least two liters of it every day, and eats like a bird, some days nothing at all. She's lost that 'joie de vivre' she once had, isn't as sociable, and her grades have dropped. This has been going on since she was sixteen. She's now a few months short of her nineteenth birthday. I've tried everything I could to help, but she doesn't seem to want to help herself. About two years ago, we discovered she had a stomach ulcer. We think it is as a result of all the soda pop, so now she's on meds for that. I've taken her to the best doctors and psychologists, but there's no sign of improvement. Over the last twelve to eighteen months, her ankles, elbows, and other joints have stiffened, and she's in pain most of the time, though I've never heard her complain. The diagnosis is rheumatoid arthritis. I'm here with you, as a last resort. I don't want to see her going into the future on crutches at such an early age. I'd give anything to have the old Helen back, and I'm sure she would, too. Can you please help?"

Before I committed to help, I wanted to meet with Helen to make sure she was open to more treatment and to seeing me because *she* wanted to, and not because her mom insisted on her coming to see me.

At our first appointment, not knowing what to expect, Helen was a more than a little nervous and wasn't prepared to tell me her story. I knew there was one. So, we talked about school, her likes, dislikes, favorite subjects, friends, and whatever else came to mind. Over a few sessions, she shared the reason for her eating disorder. One night, when her mom was on night shift at the hospital, Helen went to a party with a few girlfriends. Her mom knew she was with her best friend, but not that they were going to an unchaperoned get-together with "boys and booze". This was only the second mixed party Helen had been to, and lots of her friends were there, so she expected it to be "as much fun as the first one." Sometime during the night, after a few drinks (only two she said), a boy from her college, not in her year, started flirting with her. They danced a bit, had another drink, and then he asked if she would like to go somewhere a little less noisy to talk. They finished up in one of the upstairs bedrooms at his suggestion, and she found herself helplessly cornered. The worst happened when, after he was done, he called a couple of mates up to the room. You can imagine the rest.

The next day was Sunday, the one day of the week when Helen and her mom always tried to spend the morning together and have a huge brunch of pancakes, bacon, eggs, and the lot. That Sunday, she wouldn't get out of bed and told her mom that she'd been sick from the previous night and maybe it was something she had eaten. Still traumatized, she didn't get up for the rest of the day. Her mom fussed, made sure she was warm and comfortable, and offered different remedies to help settle her stomach.

It made Helen feel worse. "I didn't deserve being cared for; I'd lied to Mom." She decided she wouldn't tell her mom anything because they had both gone through a rough time with the divorce, and now they were happy and closer than ever. If she reported it to the police, everything would become public, and her mom would be so disappointed in her. All her friends would find out, the whole college would know. "I couldn't do it." Just the thought of it made her "panicky and physically sick." Anyway, she believed the boys would stick together, and if the truth came to light, they'd lie, or even worse, would say that Helen invited it.

She couldn't accept that none of it was her fault so wouldn't even allow herself to be angry. In the following weeks, overwhelmed by guilt, shame, and the fear that someone would discover her secret, she avoided spending time with her friends the way she used to. They had all loved to roller-skate and spent hours on the weekend competing. Since the assault, she'd stopped. When asked why by anyone, her typical response was, "I'm overwhelmed; there's so much studying to do at college. I need to buckle down and be more serious."

Soon, sadness and loneliness became Helen's new normal. She ate less and less, and began to drink liters of soda pop every day because it "gives me energy." She'd lost weight, though she had never carried any excess. In the past, Helen had been fit, healthy, and comfortable in her own skin. Since the assault, she cried a lot and become fragile and defensive if anyone tried to help her. She developed an ulcer. In constant pain from stiff ankles, elbows, and knees, walking was also a challenge. Roller-skating was now a distant memory.

However, within five months of our first meeting, a happy, healthy, arthritis-free and ulcer-free Helen was back in the roller-skating rink.

CASE NOTES   MEET MIREILLE

Mireille and I first met at my De-Mystifying Eating Disorders and Weight Loss weekend workshop. She was a sturdy, highly stressed, busy executive in her early forties, who had made the decision to finally lose those extra pounds she'd been carrying for the past decade. Sharing her story with the class, it emerged that her life had taken an unexpected turn when her younger sister and her brother-in-law had been killed in a motor vehicle accident, seven years ago, leaving their daughter, age ten, and a son, age eight, orphaned. As the sole remaining family member, Mireille was reluctant to place the children into welfare, so she decided to raise them with the support of her husband.

The couple, who were well matched in their interests and values, had decided early in their marriage that they wouldn't have children of their own, as both were committed to their respective careers and loved the lifestyle it afforded them. Taking on her sister's children was a momentous decision; one they thought they would never have to make. Neither felt they had a parental mindset or skillset, but they had always loved their niece and nephew, so they took them in with an open heart. Early in their "instant family" experience, still overwhelmed by grief, with marital life heading sideways, stress levels quickly escalated. Each wanted to keep their career, which had taken them decades to build. After some negotiation, Mireille was able to restructure her work schedule to work some days from home, allowing her to spend time with the children.

Before the tragedy, after dinner, both she and her husband enjoyed settling down at night with a packet of tortilla chips and dip to watch a movie, often with a glass of good wine. If not a movie, they would curl up in their favorite chair to read, each with their own packet of whatever they were craving. Marielle admits that she had probably started her descent, emotionally and physically, back then. The unexpected disruption to her comfortable and comforting routines, lack of privacy, and feelings of inadequacy as a mom set her firmly on the path of emotional eating. Even though she "couldn't and wouldn't have done anything different…"

After three or four years, the couple had adapted, the family unit was functioning well, and they were seemingly happy. Then, Mireille's husband managed to secure a lucrative contract away from home. He'd be gone for two or three months at a time, but they mutually agreed it would be worth it, knowing they now had the responsibility of educating the children. In his absence, she brought in a few regular hours of home-help, which allowed her to continue working full-time hours.

One morning, she woke to the realization that her husband seemed a little reluctant to come home between contracts, was not as enthused as he'd always been, nor was he as accessible via his cell. When he did make it home, he was less affectionate. "Something had broken." Rather than confronting him directly, for fear of him leaving permanently and of the financial ramifications, she plodded on. Months drifted into years. Thirty-seven pounds later, her eating habits were totally out of control, with no foreseeable way back.

What she needed initially was not another diet; she needed the courage to confront reality and speak up. Working together, during and after the workshop, we rid Mireille of every self-destructive thought, fear, and corrosive emotion she had suffered since the loss of her sister. She finally had that conversation with her husband, who admitted to having a new love in his life. She is now divorced and living comfortably with the children. Last time I saw Mireille, she had dropped almost all thirty-seven pounds and was radiantly happy.

Once you understand that eating disorders are a symptom of something far deeper, you will be better able to reach your goals and a return to optimal health. These exercises are designed to do just that. Take it slow. Be kind to yourself, not critical.

EXERCISE: FREEDOM FROM CORROSIVE EMOTIONS AND ATTRIBUTES

- Most important: please take your time with the process. Find a quiet place to be, where you are unlikely to be interrupted. Relax, take regular breaths. Slowly, read each emotion or belief to yourself at least twice, so you start to get a feel for which resonate most strongly for you. Be patient with yourself on the path to recovery. Remember, healing is a journey, not a transaction.
- If your head and heart are feeling cluttered, I recommend you return to Chapter 6, Accessing Your Creative Genius, before you go further. The guidelines and simple exercises there will best prepare you to move forward.
- To start, I suggest you reflect on your past to identify when you first started feeling distressed enough to change your relationship with food.
    - Where were you? (A specific location or different state)
    - Who were you with?
    - Was it in early childhood, teen years, or later?
    - What happened to cause you to become so distressed?
    - Were others with you helpful, or were they part of the problem?
    - How did they make you feel?
    - How often have those circumstances been repeated since then?

- What is the voice in your head saying to you and about you?

  Take your time to complete this step; it is important. Write down whatever comes to mind, regardless of whether it makes sense to you right now, because at that time, it did. Whatever happened back then to trigger this setback has become stuck in your subconscious memory and needs to be released.

- Next, free yourself of your emotional pain and unhappy memories. The following Inventory of Corrosive Emotions and Attributes, created specifically for readers with a similar history to your own, will help you identify those feelings. Write them down, and allocate a numeric rating from 0-10, using the guidelines in Chapter 7.

- Process each one that applies to your personal experience, using the script below. You can edit the underlined words to suit your needs, though it's important to keep it short and on point.

  NOTE: If you feel a little overwhelmed by the prospect of releasing those emotions, it could be that you are being sabotaged by subconscious resistance, which is fear-based. Refer to Chapter 8, which contains beliefs specific to resistance and stagnation. Process those before returning to this page.

RELEASE OF CORROSIVE EMOTIONS

I acknowledge my feelings of being inferior as an impediment to my Life goals, so now release them from their earliest point of origin, from every aspect of my life and across all dimensions of time. I am supported by the Universe in this choice.

EATING DISORDERS AND WEIGHT LOSS
CORROSIVE EMOTIONS & ATTRIBUTES

Abandoned	Disrespected	Misunderstood
Angry	Embarrassed	Neglected
Anxiety	Exhausted	Rejected
Betrayed	Fat	Sadness
Bored	Frightened	Second-Rate
Confused	Frustrated	Shame
Crushed	Grief	Stressed
Defeated	Guilt	Trapped
Depressed	Ignored	Ugly
Deprived	Impatient	Unacknowledged
Desperate	Inferior	Unfriendly
Directionless	Invisible	Unlovable
Disconnected	Isolated	Unloved
Disempowered	Loneliness	Unsafe
Disgusted	Lost	Unwelcome
Disheartened	Mean	Wounded

As you move forward, don't forget to practice self-forgiveness. The descent into self-sabotaging habits or addictive behaviors causes us to become self-critical, particularly in relation to self-image. That happens because we are subconsciously striving to live up to what we believe is "the ideal". It's healthy to have balanced, achievable goals in relation to self-image; it is not healthy to beat ourselves up consistently when we fall short. When you persistently beat yourself up for not achieving your goal, you are adding fuel to the fire. As self-criticism spirals out of control, it takes over your life, daily routines become a burden, you suffer mood swings and depression, and life becomes more complicated. Not only that, you will also still have the original issue to deal with. It's time you take a step back to regain some sort of perspective. You have the best chance of doing that once you have released the corrosive emotions keeping you stuck, and you have completed the exercise in Self-Forgiveness in Chapter 8. Then move on to the next step.

Next, we'll address the challenges which emerge from a distorted reality, a reality which is relentlessly fed by the corrosive emotions you have already identified and released. Anyone who has succumbed to an eating disorder or any other addiction, knows that their every action is controlled by that momentum. As with emotions, misguided thoughts and beliefs arise as neural pathways in your brain are impacted by stress hormones feeding your flight or fight response, and reinforced each time you re-engage addictive behavior. Gradually, you become more wary and distrusting of those closest to you and the world at large. You are constantly on high alert, defensive, and often frightened. Be assured that realignment of your thoughts and misconceptions is equally possible, and well within your control.

As a guideline, what follows is the inventory of Self-Defeating Beliefs held by many others who suffered from eating disorders and are now fully recovered.

DE-MYSTIFYING EATING DISORDERS AND WEIGHT LOSS

EXERCISE: FREEDOM FROM SELF-DEFEATING BELIEFS & MISCONCEPTIONS

- Please take your time with this part of the process. Find a quiet place to be, where you are unlikely to be interrupted. Relax, take regular breaths.
- To start, I recommend you use this list. Reading each belief a few times, slowly and mindfully, will promote a connection with your subconscious and to beliefs about yourself that you may have been suppressing for years.
- Choose those concepts which relate to your personal experience, and write them down.
- You might also discover that you are holding resentment towards anyone who you believe has directly or indirectly contributed to your addiction. If so, write down those names separately, and set that list aside for later processing. See Note at the end of this chapter.
- Next, release the beliefs you've identified using the script beneath the inventory. Edit the underlined words to suit your needs, but please remember to keep edits short and on point.

EATING DISORDERS AND WEIGHT LOSS SELF-DEFEATING BELIEFS & MISCONCEPTIONS

- I don't believe I can ever get better.
- This is just another program that won't work.
- I hate change.
- No one can help me.
- My life is an ongoing struggle.
- I can't let go of past events and sad memories.
- No matter what I do, nothing makes me feel better.
- I have no control over my life or my body.
- I need my eating disorder to stay in control of my life.
- I need to listen to the voice in my head.
- I am ashamed of myself.
- I hate my body/I am embarrassed by my body.
- I'm not good enough.
- I don't deserve better.
- I need to be different to fit in.
- I will only be accepted socially if I am thin.
- I am unloved/my parents never wanted me or loved me.
- I am past caring.
- Emotions are my enemy.
- Emotions are overwhelming.
- I can't cope with painful emotions.
- The world is an unsafe and unhappy place to be.
- I am only accepted socially if I have a partner.
- If I looked different, I would be more popular/liked/have more friends.
- If I do things perfectly every time, I'll be happier.

DE-MYSTIFYING EATING DISORDERS AND WEIGHT LOSS

- If I do things perfectly every time, I'll be less anxious.
- My eating disorder is the only way I have to express my emotions.
- It's too painful to express emotions in any other way.
- It's not possible for me to express emotions in any other way.
- I won't fit in unless I am skinny.
- The only way I am going to feel good about myself is when I am skinny.
- If I am skinny, I will be happy and successful. It's the only way.
- I am invisible/I am unimportant/I am not special.
- I am not heard.
- I am disrespected.
- I make people angry/my parents angry.
- It's my fault they are always fighting.
- It's my fault they are splitting up.
- It's my job to keep other people happy.
- I have no right to have fun.
- As a parent, my needs always have to come last.
- I am a disappointment to myself, my family, and friends.
- I can't eat in front of other people/in public.
- It's not safe for me to eat in front of other people/in public.
- I don't know what it feels like to relax around food and eating.
- If I looked different, my partner would pay more attention/ would love me more.
- I am unable to discuss my emotions and concerns with anyone.
- There's a price to pay for everything; nothing comes easy.
- I am unsupported by the Universe/Higher Power/God (or equivalent).
- Being overweight keeps me safe.
- Being overweight gives me power and presence.

RELEASE OF SELF-DEFEATING BELIEFS

The concept that <u>it sounds too simple to work</u>
no longer serves my best interests.
I release it now from every cell of my body, every
aspect of my life, and across all dimensions of time.
I am supported by the Universe in this transition.

The previous steps incorporate all the essential elements of the entire program to clear a path for the True Self to re-emerge. I've had amazing feedback from so many whose lives have been transformed simply by working through the weeding scripts. You too can join them in feeling much happier, more confident, freer, and in control of a newfound direction. No longer emotionally triggered by certain people or circumstances, they are living as creative, expressive, and joyful beings.

BONUS: SUPERCHARGED CREATIVE DOWNLOAD SCRIPTS

- Sprinkle some stardust on your newfound Self! Creative Downloads are most effective when you've processed the worst of your corrosive emotions and misguided beliefs.
- In Chapter 7, you discovered the Inventory of Life-Affirming Choices which reflects only feel-good emotions and attributes to which you might aspire. In Chapter 8, you will find the Script for Creative Downloads to replace misguided beliefs and attitudes, which work in the same way. Adding both to your toolbox will be like reprogramming your new reality on steroids. Go for it!

Note: If you have a list of people who you believe have contributed to your addictive behavior, my next suggestion is something you might consider when (and only when) you feel you have recovered and have some sense of control over your life. In Chapter 13, Advanced Integration Scripts, there's an exercise titled Forgive and Forget. I will never recommend you "force" forgiveness if you feel it's not appropriate, or not the right time, but carrying resentment, hatred, or other disempowering emotions will do you harm. So, please take a look at that if/when you're ready. Trust me when I say you'll feel freer and so much better.

Chapter 12

Embracing the Flow of Money and Abundance

Money, and what it represents, has power. It can bring out the very best in us and the worst beyond imagination. At its best, it helps us support our families and loved ones, provides access to education, and subsidizes many community and support services for the less fortunate. Further afield, it brings desperately needed food, water, and health services to remote villages and creates work and learning opportunities that were previously non-existent. At its worst, it is used to undermine political stability across the globe, has been manipulated by those in power to deprive people of their rightful quality of life, has been the cause of countless homicides, and is known to divide once-close families in the absence of a satisfactory will and testament.

Constant exposure to newsfeeds via print or social media has a subliminal effect on your own attitude towards money from your early days, particularly towards people who have heaps of it. Closer to home, you are conditioned by your birth family's financial status, perhaps going back generations. You may have been taught that the subject of money should not be spoken of, particularly if you are of British origins, or the stereotype that all Scots are thrifty. Education, pop-culture, religious and spiritual beliefs, ethnicity, and cultural norms also play a role in developing our subconscious beliefs about entitlement to money and abundance. Regardless of where they originate, how deep your financial rut, how confused you are, how low your self-expectations are, or how hopeless you feel right now, this chapter will help you generate new super-charged momentum to achieve your big-picture plans. Think *freedom to live the life you love.*

You'd likely already be wealthy if you had a dollar for every minute you ever worried about money, the lack of it, or how to get it; doubted your ability to make it; believed you don't deserve it; tried to be even more frugal with it; feared losing it or being trapped in debt; decided how to spend it; wanted more of it or simply daydreamed about what it might feel like to have more than you actually need. That really shouldn't come as a surprise, given what we learned from thought leader extraordinaire Bruce Lipton's research in Chapter 3; that is, that when it comes to how and what we think every day, our default setting revolves around scarcity and lack.

What we don't have, believe we can't have, and what could or should have been consumes around 70% of our thoughts. And we know that negative thoughts and worry generate stress hormones within our neural pathways that are reinforced each time we re-engage those thought patterns. We remain on that treadmill until we truly understand that *reprogramming the subconscious* is the only way out. That's good news for you, because you now have the tools, right here in your hands, and have already proven just how easy it is to change your outlook.

CASE NOTES   MEET TESSA

Looking at Tessa now, as a successful entrepreneur, it's hard to believe she was ever anything but wealthy and successful. Her belief systems around money and success were instilled by her parents, none of them good.

Partners in a service-based business, they'd worked long and hard to make it the success it is today. Along the way, in fact, from the very early days of the business, Tessa's mother realized she preferred playing the role of a business partner than that of being a mom. She decided to reassign her maternal responsibilities to hired help. When she was home, she made sure her three children understood, in no uncertain terms, the price she and her husband had to pay to keep them fed and educated. She openly and often stated in front of them that becoming a mom had been a huge mistake. Also, she felt none of the children had the "intelligence or common sense" to contribute to the family business, or in fact, any business. Not a warm, likable person, she thrived at work, was manipulative, and loved being in control of their few employees who mostly only tolerated her attitude from sheer financial necessity.

Her husband was typically more amenable and feared that any kind of opposition might put the business or their personal relationship at risk. Eventually, their relationship broke down, but they remained partners in the business. Each child grew to adulthood with very low self-esteem and feeling powerless, flawed, worthless, and unwanted. They each had a distorted view of money and their entitlement to it. Understandably, none believed they were capable or assertive enough to mirror their parents' success, though Tessa had now far surpassed theirs.

At our first meeting, Tessa shared her excitement at opening her own business, which after three years was slowly gathering momentum. One of her biggest challenges was negotiating client contracts in that she gave away too much too soon. People in authority intimidated her. She felt they were judging her in the same way her mother had, so inevitably she started on the back foot, almost embarrassed to be there. Rationally, it made no sense because most of her prospective clients were referred by other clients who appreciated the quality and consistency of her work. On completion of the contract, when it was time to send the invoice, she procrastinated, feeling unworthy to ask for what she was due. She also let outstanding invoices slide because she found it too difficult to call clients about them. Tessa was owed a great deal of money.

Our initial goal was to restore Tessa's sense of self-worth and confidence, and then to realign misguided beliefs around the flow of money, deservedness, and wealth. I am delighted to report a complete turnaround. Not only is Tessa now reaping the benefits of an ever-increasing cash flow, but she is also well respected as a compassionate, communicative, and supportive employer.

CASE NOTES   MEET RINA

Rina was born happy. She was one of these kids who is constantly smiling, always looking on the bright side of any situation, and who are a joy to be around. Unlike some kids, sharing came easily; her generous nature was tempered only by the reality of the poverty to which she was born. With her dad more often unemployed, or "under the weather", three meals a day were never guaranteed, nor were they expected. As a child, new clothes were a rare treat; hand-me-downs from neighbors, friends, and the local Sally Ann were the only source of her everyday wear. School texts and notebooks were treated with special care, neither battered nor accidentally lost. She made sure to arrive early enough to enjoy her free school breakfast and waited till mid-afternoon to eat whatever her mother had packed, in case there was no dinner. A diligent and respectful student, she was favored by her classmates and teachers alike and known as someone always there to help with difficult math calculations and other homework.

Fast forward. With financial support from a well-to-do relative, Rina graduated from university with honors in accounting, the only one in her family ever to have attended university. She now has a great job and her own apartment, a short transit from the office. Sounds perfect. The complication she had when we first met was that decades of scrimping, saving, and self-denial had firmly implanted the idea in her subconscious that "scarcity and lack" were forever to be her reality. She admitted that her apartment looked like a monk's cell, in a minimalist sort of way, but far from peacefully Zen. Rina shared that even though her future is secure, and she is earning well, she still shops at the local Sally Ann. She spends the least possible amount on food, or more accurately, has been conditioned from childhood to eat only enough to keep body and soul together. Needless to say, she didn't look healthy – far from it. Outside of work, life was not fun. Well-liked and often invited, she socialized as little as possible, avoiding any event that might involve what she considered to be non-essential or frivolous spending.

She was profoundly unhappy, had identified the cause, but didn't have the tools to move forward. "My only focus was to build a healthy bank balance." A great idea, but at what cost? She lived in denial of the fact that working those long hours with insufficient nourishment and self-care and being unhappy was compromising her health, and possibly worse if she persisted. And eventually, invitations would stop coming. Within a few short months of sessions, Rina's life took a turn for the better. Although still careful with her spending, she has come to a happy compromise between her habitual pattern of self-deprivation and the need to have fun and enjoy socializing. She also loves spending time in her now more comfortable, colorful abode. Her bank account continues to be robust.

When the tide starts to turn, even when evidence of the Universal flow of abundance is right in front of you, it can be difficult to accept that change has finally arrived. You are skeptical and fearful that it won't last, so you cling to what you know because it feels safe. Clinging in fear creates blocks to both the incoming and outgoing streams of money. The only way forward is to surrender to all the abundance coming your way, breathe it in, immerse yourself in it, and have fun with it.

CASE NOTES   MEET VERITY

Verity grew up in an artist colony; her mom is a sculptor, and her dad fills his time as the on-site handyman. The subject of money was rarely mentioned, if at all, in Verity's presence, nor was the word "budget", so the move to city living in her late teens was a big change. It wasn't too stressful sharing costs with two other housemates, and it helped that she was not inclined towards designer fashion or expensive restaurants. Having housemates who prodded her to be accountable for her spending also worked for a time. But as she met new friends, found a better paying job, and developed more expensive tastes, she fell into the habit of shopping with her credit card; something she had not previously done. Within a few short years, she was well behind in her payments. Her solution was to "just get another card." Press repeat.

When we spoke about that period in her life, she admitted that deep down, she expected to find someone to marry her or at least look after her – a "knight in shining armor." That didn't happen. At forty-two, she was still in debt, at an all-time low period of her life, and suffering anxiety attacks every month when it was time to pay her bills. After a few long-term relationships that ended poorly, she now lives alone, with no one to prompt her to be cautious of her spending. She jokingly referred to her spending as "retail therapy", except that it wasn't. Following a few private consultations, she came to the weekend Wealth and Abundance workshop.

The following week I received this email. *Thank you for the workshop last weekend. I really have noticed some positive shifts in my attitude toward money already... I am actually looking forward to paying my bills for a change, and I think I have managed to become friendly towards that foreign word "budget".* Fast forward. She is now living a comfortable, happy, debt-free life, albeit still single.

EXERCISE: REMOVING THE BARRIERS TO MONEY AND ABUNDANCE

- Most important: please take your time with the process. Find a quiet place to be, where you are unlikely to be interrupted. Relax, take regular breaths. Slowly, read each emotion or belief

to yourself at least twice, so you start to get a feel for which resonate most strongly for you. Be patient with yourself on the path to recovery. Remember, healing is a journey, not a transaction.
- Review your life within the context of events such as I have done with Verity, Rina, and Tessa. Document those defining moments and events, reducing the narrative for each one to bullet point format.
    - What were the circumstances you remember from childhood that first shaped your thoughts about your family's financial status?
    - How were you personally impacted during your school days?
    - If your fears and discomfort around the subject of money didn't start in childhood, when was it?
    - Have you had a recent financial crisis, or is your problem the result of cumulative spending behaviors?
    - What else has contributed to your fears or self-sabotaging behaviors?
- Your Emotional Inventory. Without exception, each person who has come to me to establish a more constructive relationship with money and abundance was undermined by multiple issues associated with low self-esteem and even lower self-expectation. So, for this next step, I recommend you return to the Corrosive Emotions and Attributes associated with identity and self-esteem in Chapter 9 to help you clarify your feelings.
- Write them down, and allocate a numeric rating from 0-10. Process each one that applies to your personal experience

using the script for Release of Corrosive Emotions. You can edit the underlined words to suit your needs, though it's important to keep it short and on point.

NOTE: If you feel a little overwhelmed by the prospect of releasing those emotions, it could be that you are being sabotaged by subconscious resistance, which is fear-based. Refer to Chapter 8, which contains beliefs specific to resistance and stagnation.

- Practice self-forgiveness. You now have a better idea of where it all started and rid yourself of the feelings keeping you stuck. You will feel more decisive and capable of moving forward with positive momentum. A shift in your emotions most often results in the same for perceptions and attitudes. But, if you are still beating yourself up, the Self-Forgiveness Script is non-negotiable. You will find it in Chapter 8. When you're ready, come back here to reprogram your beliefs and misconceptions.
- Limiting beliefs create confusion. Following is a comprehensive Inventory of Self-Defeating Beliefs and Misconceptions contributed by clients and students of Wealth and Abundance workshops. Identify those aligned to your personal experience, and then process them using the script for Releasing Self-Defeating Beliefs, which can be found below the Inventory on the next page. Add any others that may be bouncing around in your head. There's no limit to what you can do with these scripts. Go for it!

EMBRACING WEALTH AND ABUNDANCE
SELF-DEFEATING BELIEFS & MISCONCEPTIONS

- I can't cope with change.
- Change typically brings negative consequences.
- Healing and change are possible for others, but not for me.
- It's hard to let go of the past.
- I am trapped in my situation/I'll never get out from under this debt.
- I am powerless to make changes.
- Life is tough/will always be hard.
- Nothing in life comes easy.
- I am disconnected from the Universal flow of Abundance.
- There is no such thing as the Universal flow of Abundance.
- I have no control over my life.
- I hate myself/I hate my life.
- I am a loser/a failure/I am stupid.
- I am a disappointment to myself/to my family.
- Life is meant to be about pain and suffering.
- I am worthless/I don't deserve money/abundance.
- I'm not good enough to have huge amounts of money, or be abundant.
- I am incapable of handling money effectively.
- I always draw the short straw/I'm just not lucky, like other people are.
- My situation in life (or predicament) is my parents' fault.
- Success, abundance, and happiness don't last.
- Money brings overwhelming responsibility.
- If I am rich, I'll be judged, criticized.

- I am in this financial crisis because the Universe/God is punishing me.
- If I become wealthy, I know something bad will happen.
- I'll never have enough money to support my family.
- Anytime I have savings something happens to force me to spend it.
- If I ever have any real money, my family will take it from me.
- There's always a ceiling that I can't seem to go past with my savings.
- Money is elusive/I have to work hard for every cent.
- If I'm not frugal with money, I won't survive.
- It's not safe for me to have money.
- It's impossible to make serious money doing something I love.
- With money and abundance come problems.
- Money is the root of all evil.
- It's selfish (greedy) to want more money.
- If I became rich/abundant, I would lose my friends.
- People will resent me or be jealous of me having more money.
- If I became rich/abundant, it would create problems within my family.
- Most rich people are corrupt/make their money illegally.
- Rich people can't be trusted.
- Rich people have attitude/are arrogant/are elitist.
- If I became rich/abundant, everyone would hit on me for money.
- Giving is hard for me materially/financially.
- It's not right for me to have more money than my parents.
- It's not right for me to have more money than my siblings.

- I'm destined to be poor because my parents were poor, and their parents were poor.
- The Universe/God will punish me for wanting more material things.
- It's not spiritual to be wealthy and abundant.
- Poor people are closer to God.
- If the Universe/God meant for me to be wealthy, I would have been born to it.

RELEASE OF SELF-DEFEATING BELIEFS

The concept that <u>it sounds too simple to actually work</u> no longer serves my best interests. I release it now from every cell of my body, every aspect of my life, and across all dimensions of time. I am supported by the Universe in this transition.

The previous steps incorporate all the essential elements of the entire program to clear a path for the True Self to re-emerge. I've had amazing feedback from so many whose lives have been transformed simply by working through the weeding scripts. You too can join them in feeling much happier, more confident, freer, and in control of a newfound direction. No longer emotionally triggered by certain people or circumstances, they are living as creative, expressive, and joyful beings.

BONUS: SUPERCHARGED CREATIVE DOWNLOAD SCRIPTS

- Unleash your full potential! Creative Downloads are most effective when you've processed the worst of your corrosive emotions and misguided beliefs.
- In Chapter 7, you discovered the Inventory of Life-Affirming Choices, which reflects only feel-good emotions and attributes to which you might aspire. In Chapter 8, you will find the script for Creative Downloads to replace misguided beliefs and attitudes, which work in the same way. Adding both to your toolbox will be like reprogramming your new reality on steroids. Go for it!
- Try these Creative Downloads to open the flow of abundance. From the list let's take *I can't cope with change*. Instead, your Download might sound something like *I am flexible and adaptable*, or better still, *I adapt to change with ease and grace.* Here's another example: *I am a disappointment to myself, and my family* could be replaced with, *I am proud of the efforts I am making to turn things around.*
  Or as another option: *I am in transition to a debt-free, financially viable future,* or *It's okay that I have messed up; I'm human. This crisis is part of my journey to financial freedom.*

Whatever concepts resonate with your needs and direction will work. Please remember to keep the scripts short and on point.

Chapter 13

Advanced Integration Scripts

These scripts are complementary to those found elsewhere in this book and not intended to precede them or be used independently of them. Please review the scripts a few times in advance of attempting to put them into practice. Each obstacle to your progress has its own script, which should for best effect be used strictly as prescribed.

This chapter deals with shadow influences, which can alter your behavioral and response patterns, and over which you have seemingly no control. They can arise from physical and emotional incidental trauma within this life cycle or be inherited from past generations within other dimensions of time, caused by addiction, or maliciously inflicted by others. That those influences can be still impacting your day-to-day life was first proven by Dr. Lars Olov Bygren and Professor Marcus Pembrey previously introduced in Chapter 3. In general, the inherited shadow influences are in a sense benign and not inflicted upon you with harmful intent. You may be surprised to discover that other influences, far from benign, can change the trajectory of your life. We will start with the everyday situations that are most familiar and work outwards from there.

RELEASE CELLULAR SHOCK AND TRAUMA

This script is particularly useful if you are holding onto the memory of a traumatic event or have in the past suffered any kind of shock. Shock alters the vibration of the body, disrupting homeostasis sometimes indefinitely. It can happen as a result of a fall, a serious injury, having to undergo surgery, witnessing a motor vehicle accident or another traumatic incident, or anything equally distressing. Mostly, with those memories, you are unable to define specific emotional impediments as the root cause. The memory could also be triggered by a smell, color, or other element which your subconscious associates with the incident.

CASE NOTES — MEET MILDRED

Mildred, a woman in her early fifties, went through an entire surgery being able to hear the surgical team's conversations, no part of which was anything she might have expected to hear. What she expected was some exchange between themselves which focused upon her personal well-being, the progress they were making, or interaction about the task at hand. None was forthcoming. Instead, she heard conversations about last weekend's fishing trip, other sporting activities, upcoming social events, and family matters. She was shocked at what she interpreted as an insensitive approach to her well-being, even though the surgery was successful. Post-surgery she was overcome by feelings of anger, confusion, and worthlessness, which were triggered every time she thought or was asked about the surgeon, the hospital, or her surgery, which was often. Over the past eight years since the event, she has changed and become moody, irritable, and unhappy, unlike her pre-op self. It was not a surprise to discover that as a child, she felt unimportant and unappreciated.

The long-term impact of untreated shock destabilizes natural bio-rhythms and disrupts sleep patterns, causing anxiety, mood swings, and poor concentration.

EXERCISE: CELLULAR SHOCK AND TRAUMA

- To ensure the best possible outcome using the following script, the wording needs to be aligned to a specific incident. For example: "fall from the ladder," "bad cut to my finger," "hard knock to my head," "stitches to my arm." You get the idea.
- Do not focus on the actual trauma while processing the release. Doing so would merely reinforce the impact of the trauma.
- I'm sure by now there's no need for me to remind you to take time to relax, to *allow* the process to flow.
- And, to become the Observer.

When that's done, you can mentally revisit the original event to check if the body is still resonating to it. If you discover residual memory, there may be a hidden upside causing you to hold onto it. If so, refer to any of the previous scripts to support your transition. Then, revisit the source of the trauma to assess its status.

RELEASE CELLULAR SHOCK AND TRAUMA

All cellular shock and trauma generated by <u>my visit to the hospital for surgery</u> is now dissolved and released from every cell of my body, every aspect of my life, and across all dimensions of time. I am supported by the Universe in this transition.

EMPOWERMENT – SOUL FRAGMENT RETRIEVAL

Just to be clear, there's no such thing as a "soul fragment". It is an analogy I have heard frequently from within the spiritual healing fraternity, which refers to a person's fragmented energy field. I like it and use it within the same context.

Let me explain. Imagine for a minute that your soul (or life force) looks something like a mango. It is a sweet tropical fruit for those who have not had the pleasure of tasting it. It has a firm, coarse outer skin covering a softer fibrous, juicy flesh (the yummy part) and a large solid core. I use the analogy in class to suggest that, when we become disempowered by a set of circumstances or by another individual or individuals, our chi, our vital life force, and our sense of Self is eroded much like removing the fibrous flesh strip by strip (fragment by fragment) from the whole.

Loss of soul fragments can happen in many ways. You may be in a situation at work, where you are on the losing end of a power struggle with a co-worker or supervisor who is moody, unpredictable, and seems to hate you. Any interaction with that person makes you feel "less than".

ADVANCED INTEGRATION SCRIPTS

Or it could be a relative or friend. You might be a mother who has a child with a long-term illness, and in your every moment you feel his/her pain. You wish that it were you suffering instead. You have lost your sense of self, albeit lovingly, to that situation, and have become disempowered by it.

Maybe you've been through a bad break-up or divorce, which sent you to your knees, or you have been the victim of abuse such as bullying, harassment, or stalking.

In any situation where one person exerts control and manipulation over another, and you, as the victim succumb, your body, mind, and spirit are adversely affected. Later, just thinking of them has you feeling anxious, intimidated, or overwhelmed, while each time the abuser's power has been reinforced, strengthened. Abusers thrive on it. Think vampire. It is as though they have sucked the blood out of you and now control your life.

How to recover? So far, you've released the more obvious corrosive emotions attached to that person or situation and have realigned your thoughts and attitudes. Well done. You feel so much more in control, far less anxious, no longer reactive to him/her/the situation, and generally happier.

And yet, you don't feel quite as comfortable and as detached as you would like to be. There's a niggling discomfort still there. So, here's what you do.

EXERCISE: EMPOWERMENT – SOUL FRAGMENT RETRIEVAL

- Take a piece of paper, a regular letter size, or you can do this on most any device. Draw a two- to three-inch circle dead center. Draw a horizontal line across the middle of it, dividing it into two equal parts. It doesn't need to be perfect. The circle represents you as an energy field.

- Next, close your eyes, relax, and imagine your soul fragments as vibrant sparks of life-affirming energy and love. Allow that feeling or image to come to you, unforced. One of my clients saw them as chocolates, another as flowers, another as pure white snowflakes. You get the idea. Whatever comes to mind. Draw as many of those as you can fit across the top of your page *outside only the top half of your circle.* Your intention is to reclaim those.

- Close your eyes again, relax, imagine your abuser's shadow energies represented as something harmful or distasteful. Allow that to arise, also unforced. Clients have seen shards of glass, fishhooks, razor blades, oily sludge, and a range of other disgusting things. Draw those below the midline from within the circle, going towards the bottom of the page. You will be discharging those from your own energy field and cellular memory.

- The following script has proven remarkably effective, instantaneously retrieving "lost soul fragments" and discharging abusers' fragments, never to return. As Observer of the creative process, in response to the script, your interpretation of this transition will be unique to you and will represent *only soul fragments, no actual person or situation.*

- Place yourself in a comfortable, relaxed position, take regular breaths. Read the script in its entirety, then close your eyes, relax, and become the Observer. The script will encourage two things to happen.

ADVANCED INTEGRATION SCRIPTS

- First: You will see/feel representation of your soul fragments being gathered together and funneled back into the top half of the circle, which is in fact, your energy field. That may take a few minutes. Let them flow gently back to you, settling in your heart center. Often that flow starts as a huge wave or river and then eases off to a trickle, and stops completely. Only when you feel or have seen them stop completely, move on to the next bullet. (Most people begin to feel the shift at core level as soon as this part is complete.)
- Second: You are now empowered to discharge the abuser's shadow energies from inside the circle (your energy field). Likely, in your creative process, the representation of those energies will start moving out from the circle to the bottom of the page, or completely off it. This part is not complete until you feel totally free of that shadow. As in the bullet above, the release may take a few minutes. Be patient, and don't rush any part of this exercise.
- The best way to check your progress is to close your eyes, reimagine a past scenario or contact with the offender. How are you feeling? Your response should be neutral. If like most of us, there has been more than one offender, you can list those on that same sheet and state their names as you read the first part of the script. The results will include them all – awesome! NOTE: You will not need the drawing each time you use this exercise in the future, unless you prefer it, because you already have the idea and intention of it.

EMPOWERMENT - SOUL FRAGMENT RETRIEVAL

All soul fragments lost through the process of disempowerment to (state the name/s) are now retrieved, purified, and returned to my True Self. Then, all soul fragments belonging to (use "him"/"her"/or "those same offenders") are discharged from every cell of my body, every aspect of my life, and across all dimensions of time. I am empowered by the Universe in this transition.

FORGIVE AND FORGET

I decided to take some time away from work to process the aftermath of a four-day intensive workshop that had a profound impact on my consciousness. If I were a tree, those four days were like being in the middle of an earthquake: uprooted, shaken, turned upside down, and whirled around, heading skyward. When I hit the ground, I was at the same time totally exhausted and unbelievably exhilarated. So, by the following weekend, I found myself in a holiday apartment in the beautiful coastal town of Byron Bay in New South Wales, a short distance from the awe-inspiring beauty of the hinterland. Back in the day, it was unsophisticated, mellow beyond belief, and a melting pot of ex-city-dwellers looking to get off the grid, long-haired pot-smoking hippies, artists, and other creatives. It had a unique, welcoming vibe. Exactly where I needed to be.

- My only goal, other than to live in shorts, t-shirts, and no makeup for the next seven days, was to extend that period of transformation. I decided it was time to forgive my many trespassers so I could move on. After a few days of doing absolutely nothing worth mentioning, perhaps it was avoidance, I decided to commit to the process, though I'm not sure I believed it would work. Others at the workshop, who had suffered more than I could ever imagine, said that it did wonders. So why not try it?
- First, I set the stage with heaps of candles and soft meditation music, and pen and paper at hand. Then I relaxed into a short meditation and trusted the Universe to help me recall anyone who needed to be on that list. I filled over a letter-sized page with people that I had totally forgotten, even a classmate called Roslyn, a bully from my teens, and the image of her in our middle-school uniform. This was going to take a while.
- Each person had to be forgiven individually, with conscious intention, love, and compassion. Hmmm…wasn't sure I was quite there yet, but decided to continue regardless. After I read the script each time, I sat quietly, eyes closed, in my role as Observer.
- It was an exercise in patient Observation. I allowed each person to manifest in any way they came to mind, without trying to construct a scenario. The representation of forgiveness varied from person to person. Sometimes, it was a transition from substantial physical form to ethereal, darkness to light, or from one color to another. Each transition was accompanied by a sense of relief, a lightness of being.

- To close out the process, I recalled each person to mind to get a sense of any residual resentment or anger. I was surprised to discover that all I felt was a sense of compassion towards them all that I never thought possible, except for one. I repeated his a few months later with the result I had hoped for.
- Optional: When you have completed this exercise, take the list and burn it with the acknowledgment that you are releasing all negative energy associated with it into the Universe, or sending it to White Light, or your preferred representation of Higher Intelligence.

FORGIVE AND FORGET

I, (your name), forgive you (name of person), totally and unconditionally for the pain you have caused me by your words and actions. I understand your presence has served to present a lesson, which has been learned and is now complete. So, I release you from any obligation to teach me further. I also forgive myself totally and unconditionally for the role I played in our interactions. Enfolded in the Light and Love of God, my burden has been lifted; I am free to move forward.

LIMITATIONS CAUSED BY SELF-IMPOSED VOWS, OATHS, AND AGREEMENTS

You will have realized by now that destructive influences can only take hold when you are at your most vulnerable, therefore subconsciously suggestible. Here's a perfect and real example.

ADVANCED INTEGRATION SCRIPTS

CASE NOTES   MEET BARRY

Barry, an engineer, had in his mid-thirties, after a long stretch of singledom, found a partner with whom he was passionately in love. For years, it was mutual, and he was very happy. When he came for his first consultation, he looked like a walking cadaver – gaunt, depressed, dark circles under his eyes, barely managing to drag himself through the door. He had been told by his doctors he was dangerously unwell, but they could find no physical cause of it, despite all the tests. It seems that the breakup with the "love of his life" caused a spiral downwards to a deep depression. So much so, that he was prescribed six months off work to recuperate.

Already into his fourth month when we met, Barry had been to a psychiatrist and a counselor and was on meds but had not shown any noticeable improvement. We talked through the breakup and its effects. Having heard his story, I realized he was suffering the very real effects of a death wish, though he did not believe it possible. He then recalled his daily mantra, the one that was triggered by his profound pain at being rejected, the one which he repeated all day, every day, from the moment she told him she'd found someone else, and for many months following. That mantra was: "I'll die without you."

Gradually, since she left, he had lost his appetite, predictably lost over one hundred pounds, couldn't sleep, and couldn't work. First, we dealt with beliefs and misconceptions around self-worth and self-image, and then with a range of emotional impediments, some of which originated in early childhood, as you might expect. Only then we were able to clear his misguided appeal for a premature demise. Within six sessions, he was well on the way to recovery, looking forward to the next meal, gaining weight, happy to be alive, reconnecting with friends and family, and back at work.

Similar unrelated incidents of confused thinking and self-talk came from other clients with past close ties to religious and spiritual organizations, alternative lifestyle communities, and pseudo-religious sects, who divested themselves of all material and financial assets at the behest of their leaders and who had come to later regret it.

Now independent, though impoverished, they were disillusioned, conflicted, and stymied. Years of indoctrination that "poverty equates to Godliness" was now at odds with their intention to recover their financial independence and return to their previous lifestyles and mainstream population. They had taken their initial vows of poverty in good faith. It was the rock upon which their indoctrination was founded. Others from religious communities had taken a vow of celibacy, which posed challenges of a different nature; all of which we were able to overcome, I am happy to say.

Remember that the following, and other scripts in this chapter will only take permanent effect after you have completed the work in Chapters 7 and 8.

Following is the script for Release of Self-Imposed Vows and Agreements. The underlined clause is the variable.

ADVANCED INTEGRATION SCRIPTS

RELEASE OF SELF-IMPOSED VOWS AND AGREEMENTS

All vows, oaths, covenants, and agreements, binding me <u>to lives of poverty</u> are hereby dissolved from every cell of my body, every aspect of my life, and across all dimensions of time, in my highest and best interests. So be it.

NOTE: In the case of Barry, our engineer, the script would read <u>binding me to a death wish</u>.

CUTTING TIES TO RELATIONSHIPS AND SHADOW INFLUENCES

We have all been there, done that…pined for years over "the one that got away" or agonized over what you said or did wrong, even though you had apologized repeatedly for just being you, in an effort to keep the relationship together. Or, shock and horror, you dumped someone unceremoniously before realizing you had made the biggest mistake of your life.

Fast forward a few years, or many more, and here you are still pining, wishing you could start over. In fact, every time you date someone new, you consistently compare them in every way to what you believe you might have had, and the new person falls short. You have lived in that shadow way too long.

Let's take a look at another scenario. You have recently been through an acrimonious divorce and somehow can't seem to move on, can't get your life together. Your ex-partner has and is doing well. He/she is still a major presence in your reality; you are not in theirs, so really that person is just a figment of your imagination.

The extent to which these shadow influences take hold is largely dependent upon their source of origin and the intention behind them. Conscious, malicious intention does real harm. It is very often difficult to separate yourself because the shadow belongs to someone you love or who you have depended upon by necessity.

CASE NOTES   MEET LILLIAN

Lillian is the only child of a single mom. She never knew her dad. Lillian's mom, Ruby, and her uncle were also raised by her single grandmother, whose husband died within a few years of their marriage. Grandmother Florence was a strict disciplinarian, as was her own mother. Their home was devoid of warmth, love, and laughter. She ruled the household in the best way she knew how, demanded obedience, and kept the children to very tight schedules for meals, bathing, homework, and chores. If they were not at the breakfast table by 7:30, washed and dressed for school, they were deprived of their breakfast. The same rigid routines applied to completion of weekly household chores and bath night. Sometimes as punishment, the children were forced to sleep on the hard floor instead of their bed. Punishments mostly involved some form of deprivation, rather than physical abuse, although the potential of it was always threatened. Any request for a second helping at the dinner table was ignored. Christmas and Thanksgiving went by unnoticed; birthdays were acknowledged, but not celebrated. All of this was done to lessen the risk of the children becoming spoilt and unmanageable. That same approach was adopted by Ruby in her parenting of Lillian.

Now with two children of her own, Lillian was trying to find a "better way of doing things, a different parenting style," though she had no idea of how to go about it. She could see that other moms at kindergarten had a more relaxed attitude than her own and encouraged more interaction and play than she had ever been allowed.

It didn't help Lillian that both her mom and gran were always on the sidelines giving direction, criticizing, and urging her to maintain their strict disciplinary standards. Though Lillian had hated the rigor and deprivation of her childhood, she loved and respected her mother, and intellectually, if not emotionally, understood the reasoning behind it.

Fearful of her grandmother's wrath, Lillian was finding it impossible to step out from under their shadow. She worried that if she did, she would become alienated from her mom. That was the last thing she wanted. Fast forward to present day. Lillian is happy, much more relaxed and flexible in her parenting approach, and free of the negative emotional ties imposed by her own mom and gran.

CASE NOTES   MEET ALEJANDRO

Alejandro was born and raised until his twenty-fourth year in a faraway country, which still embraces the practice of shamanism and witchcraft. Both were practiced by different members of both his ancestral and existing family. He now lives with his younger sister in North America. They are the only family members to abandon their cultural roots and are excited by the prospect of a fresh start and an escape from the fear and malevolence they had known since childhood. In spite of their self-imposed exile, the siblings miss their parents and close community ties, even though they have found new friends. Overall, they're both happy in their new life, and for the first time, each has a steady income.

It came as no surprise to me that Alejandro believed his parents and two other siblings were attempting to draw him back home through the use of curses, spells, hexes, and other rituals. He felt the weight and the consequences of them every day. In his own experience of *foresight* and *magic*, he saw his future clearly defined in North America, accompanied by all the familiar symbols representing a peaceful, happy life. He saw the same for his sister.

He had no wish to completely sever ties with his family; he loved them. He needed them to respect his choice and release him to his chosen path without penalty. Reinforcing the concept of an individual Self, separate from and independent of family members and the occult traditions that bound him, was key to his transition. We first dealt with his emotional inventory, then close to last, he completed the following exercise.

EXERCISE: CUTTING TIES TO RELATIONSHIPS AND SHADOW INFLUENCES

It's important that you read through the entire section before you start this exercise, as it is with all the others in this chapter.

This exercise can be used to either: 1) emerge from someone's shadow (their negative traits and influence) or to 2) sever a relationship completely. It's your choice; your intention will support the transition.

- Take a piece of regular letter-size paper. Grab a pen, insert a vertical line down the middle of the page, from top to bottom.

On the left side at the top insert your name, and on the right side, the name of the person whose shadow you need to escape, the Offender.

- Under your name, write a list of the things to which *you* are aspiring. Recall Lillian, who wanted to be a better parent. She wanted to be more present for her children, more open, more overtly affectionate, more patient with them, a better listener, have more fun, and be open to having other children in her home. You get the idea.
- Under the Offender's name write down your experience/ or impressions of that person, as much as you can think of. Lillian's mom (and her grandmother) was mean spirited, bitter, resentful (of being a single mom), frustrated, sad, critical, and so on.
- Sit somewhere quiet, relax, and breathe easily. Imagine you are on the platform of a train station, sitting peacefully and happy. Within you and surrounding you as an auric field are all the intentions and attributes listed under your name. You feel radiant and powerful, self-assured.
- The Offender enters the platform and stands a distance from you, not necessarily facing you. In and around that person, you can see or feel all those attributes listed under his/her name. As the Offender turns in your direction, you see that nothing has changed, coldness and bitterness (or other disturbing qualities) are etched onto their face. You are blessed with insight and able to see the invisible ties that bind you to each other. They may present as steel rods, huge chains, barbed wire, live electrical cable, or as a gossamer-fine spider web, steely strong. Allow that image to arise unforced.

- A train whistles to a stop in front of you. Your aura has become even more radiant, you feel no resentment towards the Offender, just the overwhelming sense of Universal love, acceptance, and compassion. The Offender gets on board, you remain as you are.
- Alongside the script, the rest of this visualization is an essential part of your transition to now engage in. Please read through the entire section before you start this exercise.
- Your visualization: Your offender finds a seat at the window and stares back at you as the train sets off in slow motion, really slow motion. You are not disturbed by it; you are merely the Observer. The ties that bind you are still visible, connected and strong, stretching across the distance between you. Your purpose is to transmit wave after wave of Universal love, compassion, and understanding in his or her direction as beautifully colored light. As the train moves out in slow motion, you keep watch of his/her face or energy field, until it very slowly fades into the distance, no longer visible. The ties that were binding also fall away. It is important that you take your time to watch the train slowly disappearing in the distance. If the Offender is a family member, for example, you likely have years of disharmony or conflict to release from your cellular memory. Observe patiently, until you feel a sense of calm, a sense of release, or better still, joy!

ADVANCED INTEGRATION SCRIPTS

EMERGING FROM SHADOW INFLUENCES

All shadow influences, curses, invocations, and similar instruments inflicted upon me by others, binding me to <u>lives of dependence, servility, and submission</u> are hereby dissolved from every cell of my body, every aspect of my life, and across all dimensions of time. I am supported by the Universe in this transition.

If, on the other hand, you would like to rid yourself of a person's energetic presence in your life completely, for example, the one who got away, a not-so-kind friend, or anyone else you need to let go of, then use the following script. The visualization or feeling experience as Observer will be identical, though your words and intention are different.

CUTTING TIES TO RELATIONSHIP

I acknowledge that your presence in my life has in earlier times been beneficial, and hope you have likewise benefited from our connection. For me, its relevance has come to an end; I am moving on. I release you now with love and compassion and wish you well on your journey. The tie is broken. I am free. I am supported by the Universe in this choice.

Clients report seeing the facial expression and demeanor of the Offender soften slightly, or completely change, some even smiled as the train moves out of sight. Others have had direct feedback from the person concerned that they now feel an emotional and energetic distance between them. That's fine. Well done!

The scope of these transformative practices is limited only by your imagination. Whatever the objective, it's easy to modify any of the Wise Words scripts to meet your needs, keeping the underlined elements short and on point for best effect.

Be awesome! You now know that your potential is limited only by your perceptions and choices, and that you are creative, curious, and joyful by nature. I am proof positive of someone who has created a life well beyond anything I could have imagined using these tools. My work and my life continue to be vibrant, productive, and meaningful. I wholeheartedly want the same for you and your loved ones.

In closing this chapter, I leave you with this reminder from Walt Disney: "All our dreams can come true, if we have the courage to pursue them."

Chapter 14

Our World of Oneness

Congrats are in order! You've been persistent and successful in achieving new goals and a vibrant, meaningful life. I hope you've been celebrating milestones along the way. It isn't always easy to step up and take responsibility for past choices. For me, it was way too embarrassing to admit I had been so gullible, making the same self-sabotaging choices time after time, hoping for a different outcome. At the beginning of my transition, by way of a silver lining, I learned an important lesson. It was to stop taking blame for things beyond my control. From early childhood, with no proper familial role models, I was stunted and grew into my teens and adulthood with the emotional intelligence of a gnat. So, of course there were going to be consequences, some dire. I moved through them. I learned that being empowered means to take responsibility for what is mine and to be kindly expressive and authentic instead of over-accommodating to others, hoping for their approval. Now, I see evidence of unconditional love and support surrounding me every day and too many unexpected blessings from the Universe to mention.

At the beginning of this journey, I promised a paradigm shift. And I have delivered. New ways of thinking and doing are challenging for most people, believing that anything outside their comfort zone cannot be trusted. Despite their fears, I believe without any reservation the time will come in the not-too-distant future when humankind again embraces its inherent beauty, creative intelligence, resilience, and healing capability. We will, in that New Age, be able to flourish without dependence on harmful, human-made substances and band-aid solutions.

"All truth passes through three stages.
First, it is ridiculed. Second, it is violently opposed.
Third, it is accepted as self-evident."
Arthur Schopenhauer

Your transition is proof of what is possible.

- You have proven that thoughts and emotions are fluid and malleable over time and space, that re-engineering is possible.
- You understand that creative consciousness is all you need to access the infinite source of Universal Abundance that surrounds us all.
- You are no longer a victim or merely a passive observer.
- You have acquired emotional resilience as an individualized, expressive, empowered Self.
- Your thoughts and actions are now inspired by those of unity, love, and compassion towards all living creatures.

- You live an authentic life, with ease and grace, in harmony with the flow of Infinite Potential, with an open heart and a clear mind.
- You are a shining light, an inspiration to others seeking a way forward.

NEW BEGINNINGS

My sole purpose in writing this book is to help shift collective consciousness to new heights and to create more positive change in the world. I ask that you join me in this effort to keep the momentum going. No doubt you have friends, family, co-workers, and avid readers in your book-club who spring immediately to mind. Please share the experience of your own transition, or pass along this book and suggest it may be helpful. When I started doing this work, I wanted to "heal" everyone. I was so enthusiastic that I became a pain in everyone's butt! I learned it's not our job to "fix" everyone, no matter how badly we want to help. And, although we live in a world of Oneness, energetically connected, for each of us, healing is a personal journey subject to multiple real-time and Universal influences and what I refer to as "Divine timing". Sometimes it's enough to plant the seed and wait for the sunshine.☺

All manner of resources is at our fingertips, literally. Just about everybody everywhere has access to an online connection, but not everyone has family and friends to rely on in times of need, or even just to share defining events in their life. Setting up a friends' group on any site such as Instagram, YouTube, Facebook, Twitter, or Snapchat is an effective way to help and connect with those needing encouragement and support. Even a short Zoom or Facetime chat. Giving support can be as simple as helping someone clarify their thoughts or to see their issue through an independent lens. Other times, it's just the right word at the right time. If you, like many students of my workshops, enjoy a more direct connection, a Saturday afternoon *calming tea and cookie meetup* can work wonders. These tools are easy to learn and share in groups and with self-improvement seekers, mind-body-spirit devotees, and emotional support groups.

In any way you can, I urge you to share your joy, encourage a mindful lifestyle, and spread love and healing for the benefit of all beings. Practitioners and workshop facilitators will find more information on the following page.

I look forward to hearing about your own experiences and transitions. You can reach me at https://www.deannaloterzo.com/contact. Included on the site are other resources you might find interesting and useful going forward.

Namaste
Deanna LoTerzo

PS: You may have bought this book on the recommendation of a family member, friend, or colleague, and most likely from on online source. If so, you know how important it is to have this book rated particularly on sites such as Amazon. If you have had a life-altering experience, or in any other way benefitted from this book, I humbly ask that you post it on social media. Help the world become a kinder, more enlightened place for us all to live in harmony. Heartfelt thanks and blessings.

For Practitioners and Workshop Facilitators

Bright Mind, Happy Heart Workshops / Courses

When you've mastered both basic and advanced processes and would like to take your own and others' well-being to a whole new level, please consider teaching the program. It's healing, enlightening and liberating for participants, and it can be fun for you. More important is that it is simple and its safe. While you are raising collective consciousness, you can also significantly increase your income and expand your patient/client base. I've done it successfully for almost two decades though am now retired from facilitation.

Clients and participants of past workshops, motivated to expand other hearts and minds, have included counselors, psychotherapists, psychologists, naturopathic & allopathic doctors, educators, nurses, Reiki Masters and other complementary health practitioners.

The book includes the entire program, best taught in two segments. Wholly experiential, it provides participants with the opportunity to engage emotionally, intellectually and creatively to accelerate their own transformation and to support others. Segment 1: Introduction; includes the core work through Chapter 9. On completion of this segment, typically, each individual has a thorough understanding of the process and the confidence to continue practice or support others beyond the workshop / course setting. Segment 2: Advanced recaps core elements of the basic program then goes on to cover the remaining chapters through 14.

The following themed workshops, covering basic principles integral to Chapters 1- 9 have proven popular. Note: there is no fee payable by you to me, or cost to you for providing these workshops or courses, other than the book you have read.

- De-mystifying Eating Disorders & Weight Loss
- Living the Dream – Wealth & Abundance
- Heart to Heart: Creating Love & Healthy Relationships
- The Creative Power of Mind, Emotion & Quantum Energy

Shine your light. My hope and dream is that you accept the challenge to teach others how to become emotionally whole and independent and to take personal responsibility for their health, their future, and that of generations to come.

SUPPORT: I am available to assist you in any way I can. Initial contact should be made via www.deannaloterzo.com/contact

Namaste
Deanna LoTerzo

Resources

CHAPTER 3

Dr. Lars Olov Bygren
http://www.umu.se/sok/english

Professor Marcus Pembrey, FMedSci, Emeritus Professor of Pediatric Genetics at the Academy of Medical Sciences, UK Bio News: https://www.bionews.org.uk/page_5518

The National Genome Research Institute:
https://www.genome.gov/12011239/a-brief-history-of-the-human-genome-project

Bruce Lipton, Ph. D., internationally renowned cell biologist and a pioneer in the new science of epigenetics. Author: *The Biology of Belief – 10th Anniversary Edition* (2015)
https://www.brucelipton.com/

Sylvia Claire (& William Novak), heart transplant recipient. Author: *A Change of Heart* (1997)

Paul Pearsall, Ph.D. (1942-2007), well-credentialed psychologist and psychoneuroimmunologist who studied heart transplant patients. His 1998 publication, *The Heart's Code – Tapping the Wisdom and Power of our Heart Energy*, contends that "the human heart, not the brain, holds the secrets that link mind, body, and spirit." www.paulpearsall.com

CHAPTER 4

Norman Doidge, M.D., psychiatrist, psychoanalyst, and researcher at Columbia University and the University of Toronto. Author: *The Brain That Changes Itself* (2007). http://www.normandoidge.com

Daniel G. Amen, M.D., clinical neuroscientist, psychiatrist, Distinguished Fellow of the American Psychiatric Association. Author: *Making a Good Brain Great* (2005)
http://danielamenmd.com/

Dr. Alvaro Pascual-Leone, Professor of Neurology, Harvard University
https://mbb.harvard.edu/people/alvaro-pascual-leone

Dawson Church, Ph.D., integrative healthcare researcher. Author: *Mind to Matter* (2018)
www.dawsonchurch.com

Loretta G. Breuning, Ph.D. Author: *Habits of a Happy Brain* (2016)
https://www.psychologytoday.com/ca/experts/loretta-g-breuning-phd

RESOURCES

Natasha Turner, ND. New York Times Best Selling Author: *The Hormone Diet (2011)* and *The Supercharged Hormone Diet* (2013)
https://drnatashaturner.com/

CHAPTER 5

Dr. Masaru Emoto, scientist and New York Times Best Selling Author: *The Hidden Messages in Water* (2005)
https://thewellnessenterprise.com/cmoto/
http://whatthebleep.com/water-crystals/

CHAPTER 7 AND 8

Bruce Lipton, Ph.D., internationally renowned cell biologist and a pioneer in the new science of epigenetics. Author: *The Biology of Belief – 10th Anniversary Edition* (2015)
https://www.brucelipton.com/

Pam Grout, Author of sixteen books, plays, and a television series and writes for *People Magazine* and *Huffington Post*. Author: *E-Squared* (2013)
www.pamgrout.com

Dr. Joe Dispenza, neuroscientist, lecturer, and New York Times Best Selling Author: *You Are the Placebo* (2014)
www.drjoedispenza.com

CHAPTER 9

David Brooks is a columnist for the *New York Times*, commentator on the *PBS NewsHour*, and author of the #1 New York Times Best Seller: *The Social Animal* (2012)

CHAPTER 10

Patricia Evans, a highly acclaimed interpersonal communications specialist and public speaker has appeared on *Oprah*, CNN, and national radio. Author: *The Verbally Abusive Relationship – How to Recognize It and How to Respond* (extended third edition 2010) www.verbalabuse.com

Robin Stern, Ph.D. is the Associate Director of the Yale Center for Emotional Intelligence and a psychoanalyst in private practice. Author: *The Gaslight Effect: How to Spot and Survive the Hidden Manipulation that Others Use to Control Your Life* (2018) http://ei.yale.edu/person/robin-stern-ph-d/

Lundy Bancroft is a workshop facilitator, consultant, and author of numerous books. He specializes in the field of domestic abuse and child maltreatment. His book *Why Does He Do That? Inside the Minds of Angry and Controlling Men* (2002) is a comprehensive look at the behaviors of abusive men. www.lundybancroft.com

About the Author

Deanna LoTerzo, an Italo-Australian by birth, has been a life coach, psychotherapist, and spiritual mentor for over 18 years. Her passion to reshape hearts, minds and attitudes to create a happier, healthier world, is unwavering. Milestones in her transition from workaholic frenzy in business management to meditative calm include seven months spent in Nepal filled with the "most amazing and unpredictable experiences and insights." Soon after, pulled to a new life in Canada, Deanna swapped her hearty European diet and buttery French croissants for veganism, and converted from relentless researcher to writer. She wakes every day with an unbridled enthusiasm for life on Vancouver Island, in beautiful British Columbia.

www.deannaloterzo.com

Printed in Canada